Table of Contents

List of Illustrations

List of Tables

List of Acronyms and Abbreviations

21 MRUUV	21-inch Mission Reconfigurable UUV
ACINT	Acoustic Intelligence
ACOMMS	Acoustic Communications
ACR	Area Coverage Rate
ADC	Association of Diving Contractors International, Inc.
ADCAP	Advanced Capability
ADS	Advanced Deployable Systems
AMPHIB	Amphibious Warfare Ship
AO FNC	Autonomous Operations Future Naval Capability
AoA	Analysis of Alternatives
AOA	Amphibious Operating Area
ARL	Applied Research Laboratory
ASDS	Advanced Swimmer Delivery System
ASN/RDA	Assistant Secretary of the Navy for Research, Development & Acquisition
ASW	Anti-Submarine Warfare
AT/FP	Anti-Terrorism/Force Protection
ATR	Automatic Target Recognition
ATV	All-Terrain Vehicle
BPAUV	Battlespace Preparation Autonomous Undersea Vehicle
BSP	Battlespace Preparation
C3	Command, Control, Communications
C4ISR	Command, Control, Communications, Computers, Intelligence, Surveillance, and Reconnaissance
CAC	Computer-Aided Classification
CAD	Computer-Aided Detection
CAI	Computer-Aided Identification
CAPTOR	Encapsulated torpedo ASW mine (MK 60)
CBNRE	Chemical, Biological, Nuclear, Radiological, and Explosives
CN3	Communication/Navigation Network Nodes

CNA	Communication/Navigation Aid
CNO	Chief of Naval Operations
COA	Carrier Operating Area
COE	Concept of Employment
COMINT	Communications Intelligence
COMM	Communications
Con	Contacts
CONOPS	Concept of Operations
COTS	Commercial-Off-the-Shelf
CSG	Carrier Strike Group
CUP	Common Undersea Picture
DADS	Deployable Autonomous Distributed System
DCIN	Detect, Classify, Identify, Neutralize
DoD	Department of Defense
EDC	Environmental Data Collection
ELINT	Electronics Intelligence
EMATT	Expendable Mobile ASW Training Target
EOD	Explosive Ordnance Disposal
ESG	Expeditionary Strike Group
EXW	Expeditionary Warfare
FNC	Future Naval Capability
GCCS-M	Global Command & Control System - Maritime
GIG	Global Information Grid
GPS	Global Positioning System
GWOT	Global War on Terrorism
HAUV	Hovering Autonomous Undersea Vehicle
HLD	Homeland Defense
HSI	Human Systems Integration
HWV	Heavy Weight Vehicle
IAW	In Accordance With
ID	Identify

IEEE	Institute for Electrical & Electronics Engineers
IER	Information Exchange Requirements
IMINT	Imagery Intelligence
INFOSEC	Information Security
IO	Information Operations
IOC	Initial Operational Capability
IPB	Intelligence Preparation of the Battlespace
IPL	Image Processing Library
ISLAMM	Improved Submarine Launched Mobile Mine
ISR	Intelligence, Surveillance & Reconnaissance
JC2	Joint Command & Control
JHU/APL	Johns Hopkins University Applied Physics Laboratory
JTRS	Joint Tactical Radio System
L&R	Launch & Recovery
LCS	Littoral Combat Ship
LD MR UUV	Large Displacement Mission Reconfigurable UUV
LMRS	Long-term Mine Reconnaissance System
LOS	Line of Sight
LR	Long Range
LSC	Littoral Sea Control
LWV	Light Weight Vehicle
MASINT	Measurement and Signature Intelligence
MCM	Mine Countermeasures
MCS	Mission Control System
MEDAL	Mine Warfare and Environmental Decisions Aids Library
METOC	Meteorology and Oceanography
MIW	Mine Warfare
MODLOC	Miscellaneous Operational Details, Local Operations (Operating Area)
MOSS	Mobile Operational Submarine Simulator
MP	Man Portable
MRD	Maritime Reconnaissance Demonstration

MTS	Marine Technology Society
NAV	Navigation
NAVMETOCCOM	Naval Meteorology and Oceanography Command
NAVOCEANO	Naval Oceanographic Office
NLW	Non-lethal Weapon
NMRS	Near-term Mine Reconnaissance System
NRAC	Naval Research Advisory Committee
NSW	Naval Special Warfare
NSWC	Naval Surface Warfare Center
NTT	Non-Traditional Tracking
NUWC	Naval Undersea Warfare Center
NWDC	Navy Warfare Doctrine Command
ONR	Office of Naval Research
OPAREA	Operations Area
ORE	Operational Readiness Evaluation
OSD	Office of the Secretary of Defense
OSI	Object Sensing and Intervention
PA	Program Arrangement
PALACE	Profiling Autonomous Lagrangian Circulation Explorer
PEO LMW	Program Executive Officer for Littoral and Mine Warfare
PEO MUW	Program Executive Officer for Mine and Undersea Warfare
PLD	Payload Delivery
PUMA	Precision Underwater Mapping (Submarine Sonar System)
RDS	Remote Deployable System
RDT&E	Research, Development, Test and Evaluation
REMUS	Remote Environmental Monitoring Units (UUV)
RF	Radio Frequency
RMS	Remote Minehunting System
ROE	Rules of Engagement
ROV	Remotely Operated Vehicle
SAHRV	Semi-Autonomous Hydrographic Reconnaissance Vehicle

SAMS	Subsurface Autonomous Mapping System
SAS	Synthetic Aperture Sonar
SATCOM	Satellite Communications
SEID	Specific Emitter Identification
SCM	Search, Classify, Map
SDV	Seal Delivery Vehicle
SIGINT	Signal Intelligence
SLOC	Sea-Line of Communication
SOF	Special Operations Forces
SP21	Sea Power 21
SSBN	Ballistic Missile Submarine
SSGN	Guided Missile Submarine
SSN	Attack Submarine
STOM	Ship to Objective Maneuver
STT	Submarine Track and Trail
SW	Shallow Water
SWARM	Shallow Water Autonomous Reconnaissance Vehicle
T-AGS	Oceanographic Survey Ship Class
TBD	To Be Determined
TCS	Time Critical Strike
TDA	Tactical Decision Aid
TEMPALT	Temporary Alterations
TLRs	Top Level Requirements
TMA	Target Motion Analysis
TRL	Technology Readiness Level
TTS	Through-the-Sensor
TTP	Tactics, Training, and Procedure
UAV	Unmanned Aerial Vehicle
UCAV	Unmanned Combat Aerial Vehicle
USS	Undersea Search and Survey
USSP	Unmanned System Strategic Plan

USV	Unmanned Surface Vehicle
USV MP	Unmanned Surface Vehicle Master Plan
UUV	Unmanned Undersea Vehicle
UUVMP	Unmanned Undersea Vehicle Master Plan
UV	Unmanned Vehicle
UXO	Unexploded Ordnance
UXV	Unmanned Vehicle (air, ground, surface or underwater)
VID	Visual Identification
VSW	Very Shallow Water

Navy UUV Master Plan
Executive Summary

The growing use of unmanned systems – air, surface, ground, and underwater is continually demonstrating new possibilities that can assist our naval forces maintain maritime superiority around the world.

Figure ES-1. UUVs at War.

Sea Power 21 specifies the use of unmanned vehicles as force multipliers and risk reduction agents for the Navy of the future and postulates a host of specific missions for which UUVs are uniquely qualified. The long-term UUV vision is to have the capability to: (1) deploy or retrieve devices, (2) gather, transmit, or act on all types of information, and (3) engage bottom, volume, surface, air or land targets (See Figure ES-2).

This Master Plan Update builds on the 2000 UUV Master Plan, updating missions, approaches, and technical and programmatic recommendations based on changes in Navy guidance, technology, platforms, and other factors since April 2000. The objectives of this Master Plan Update are to define UUV capabilities consistent with Sea Power 21, establish levels of performance for each capability, and to recommend the appropriate vehicle classes and technology investments required to efficiently achieve these recommended capabilities.

As a result of the surveys, expert panels, and analyses performed during this Master Plan update, nine high-priority UUV missions where identified that support the four Sea Power 21 Pillars. The nine missions (or UUV "Sub-Pillars"), in priority order, are:

- Intelligence, Surveillance, and Reconnaissance (ISR)
- Mine Countermeasures (MCM)
- Anti-Submarine Warfare (ASW)
- Inspection / Identification
- Oceanography
- Communication / Navigation Network Nodes (CN3)
- Payload Delivery
- Information Operations (IO)
- Time Critical Strike (TCS)

To address the nine Sea Power 21 Sub-Pillar capabilities, this Master Plan Update recommends evolving towards four general vehicle classes: Man Portable (approximately 25 to 100+ lbs displacement), Light Weight (approximately 500 lbs displacement), Heavy Weight (approximately 3000 lbs displacement), and Large (approximately 20,000 lbs displacement).

This document also makes the following recommendations:

- Continued development of UUV Standards and Modularity
- Investment in the critical technologies of autonomy, energy and propulsion, sensors and sensor processing, communications/navigation, and engagement/intervention
- Increased experimentation with UUV technologies, and
- Introduction of UUV systems into the fleet, as soon as possible.

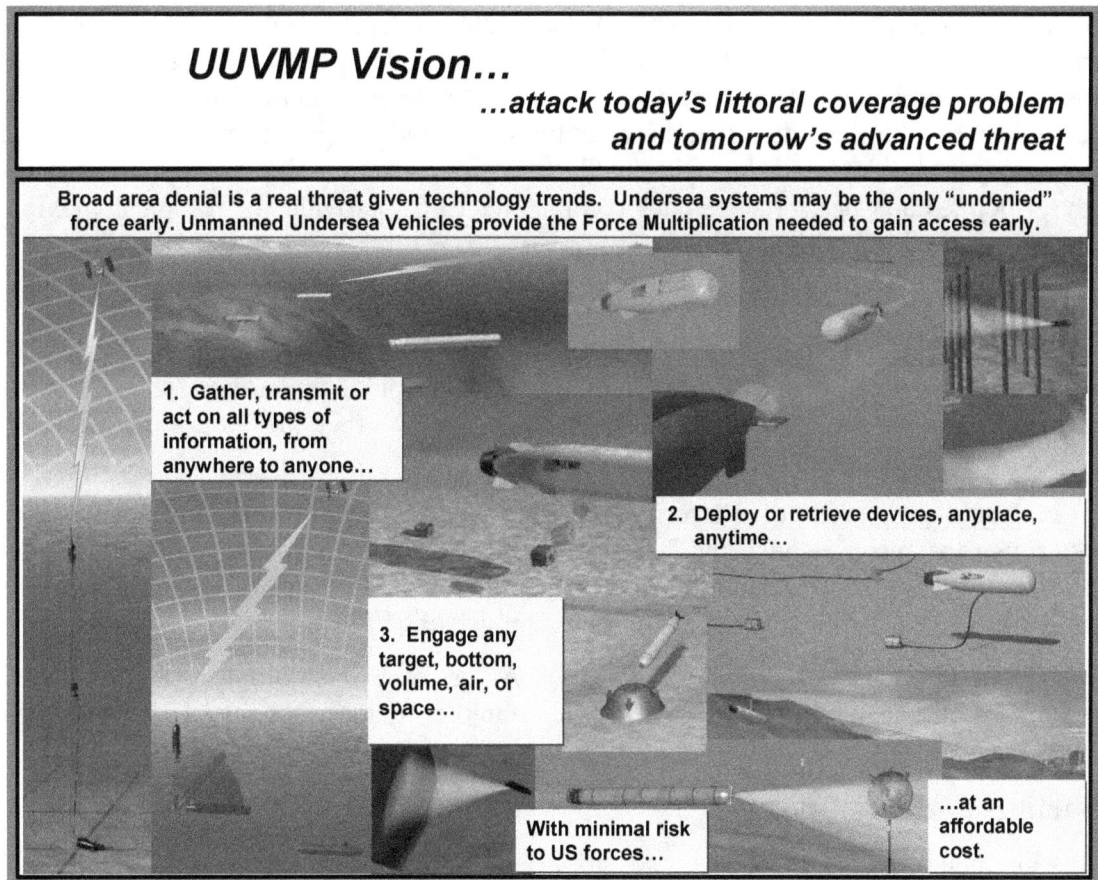

Figure ES-2. UUV Master Plan Vision

The Vision for UUVs and the Objective of the UUV Master Plan

Today our naval forces enjoy maritime superiority around the world and find themselves at a strategic inflection point during which future capabilities must be pondered with creativity and innovation. Change must be embraced and made an ally in order to take advantage of emerging technologies, concepts, and doctrine; thereby preserving the nation's global leadership. Sea Power 21 has additionally specified unmanned vehicles as force multipliers and risk reduction agents for the Navy of the future. Transformation applies to *what* we buy as well as *how* we buy and operate it–all while competing with other shifting national investment priorities.

The growing use of unmanned systems–air, surface, ground, and underwater is continually demonstrating new possibilities. While admittedly futuristic in vision, one can conceive of scenarios where UUVs sense, track, identify, target, and destroy an enemy–all autonomously and tie in with the full net-centric battlespace. UUV systems will provide a key undersea component for FORCEnet, contributing to an integrated picture of the battlespace.

Even though today's planners, operators, and technologists cannot accurately forecast the key applications for UUVs in the year 2050, this plan provides a roadmap to move toward that vision. Pursuit of this plan's updated recommendations beginning in the year 2004, will place increasingly large numbers of UUVs in the hands of warfighters. Thus,

UUVs can begin addressing near-term needs while improving understanding of mid- to far-term possibilities. Even the most futuristic applications can evolve in a confident, cost-effective manner. This confidence is based on several factors: the Sea Power 21 Sub-Pillar capabilities identified here address a broad range of user needs; critical technologies are identified that will enable tomorrow's more complex applications; and key principles and best practices are recommended that provide for a logical, flexible, and affordable development effort.

The objectives of this Master Plan are to:

Define UUV Capabilities needed in the near, mid and far term. These include mission descriptions and priorities, a high level concept of operations (CONOPS) for each, and assessment of candidate capabilities as to whether they are appropriate for UUVs (or should be assigned to other unmanned assets).

Establish Levels of Performance and a "Class" for each UUV capability. Determine the recommended number of classes of vehicles required to effectively and efficiently accomplish the recommended capabilities. In addition, examine the level of modularity and commonality that should be established within and between classes.

Evaluate UUV Technology Needs. Assess our technological readiness and recommend the technology investments that should be made to enable the development of vehicles and payloads to accomplish the recommended UUV capabilities.

Background

This document is consistent with and amplifies the challenges of the April 2000 UUV Master Plan (UUVMP), its predecessors, and successors:

- 1994: Navy UUV Program Plan (N87)–focused on immediate needs for clandestine mine reconnaissance from submarines (Near-Term Mine Reconnaissance System (NMRS) first priority, Long-Term Mine Reconnaissance System (LMRS) second priority and Tactical Oceanography third priority) with minor updates in 1995 and 1997

- April 2000: UUV Master Plan (ASN/RDA) – future focus, other missions and users

- June 2002: Small UUV Strategic Plan (PEO MUW) – Linked to UUVMP, added detail for Explosive Ordnance Disposal (EOD), Very Shallow Water (VSW) Mine Countermeasures (MCM) and Shallow-water MCM

Significant portions of the 2000 plan are now well on the way to completion. Although the 2000 plan did not espouse any particular program or technical implementation, the Navy and other developers have made strides toward making all four of the former signature capabilities a reality.

Since 2000, additional studies have been performed that provide guidance. This guidance included assessments not only of the role of UUVs, but also of the operational effectiveness of various sizes and configurations of UUVs in missions of high interest to the Navy. Those plans and studies include the studies associated with the 21" Mission Reconfigurable UUV (21 MR UUV), the Analysis of Alternatives (AoA) for the Large

Displacement UUVs (LD MR UUV), the SSGN Sensors and Payloads Study and several Naval War College and Navy Warfare Development Command studies and war games. A complete listing of documents referenced is provided in Appendix A. This UUV Master Plan Update builds on the 2000 UUV Master Plan, updating the missions, approaches, and technical and programmatic recommendations based on changes in Navy guidance, technology, employment platforms, and other factors since April 2000.

Approach

The first stage in developing the Master Plan was to generate a comprehensive pool of emerging UUV missions. To do this, several techniques were employed including field surveys, expert panels, and analysis. A series of three workshops was held to gather inputs from Navy users, stakeholders, Navy laboratories, academia, and industry. The missions were then analyzed and prioritized in accordance with Fleet and national needs. The resulting prioritized list of missions was:

- Intelligence, Surveillance and Reconnaissance (ISR)
- Mine Countermeasures (MCM)
- Anti-Submarine Warfare (ASW)
- Inspection / Identification
- Oceanography
- Communication / Navigation Network Nodes (CN3)
- Payload Delivery
- Information Operations (IO)
- Time Critical Strike (TCS)
- Barrier Patrol (Homeland Defense, Anti-Terrorism / Force Protection)
- Barrier Patrol (Sea Base support)

Following additional analysis of the suitability of UUVs for the missions, the two barrier patrol missions were deleted from those to be considered in the plan, as they are more effectively achieved via other means.

Sea Power 21 Sub-Pillar Capabilities

The high-priority missions were then grouped under the four Sea Power 21 pillars: Sea Shield, Sea Strike, Sea Base, and FORCEnet, as shown in Figure ES-3.

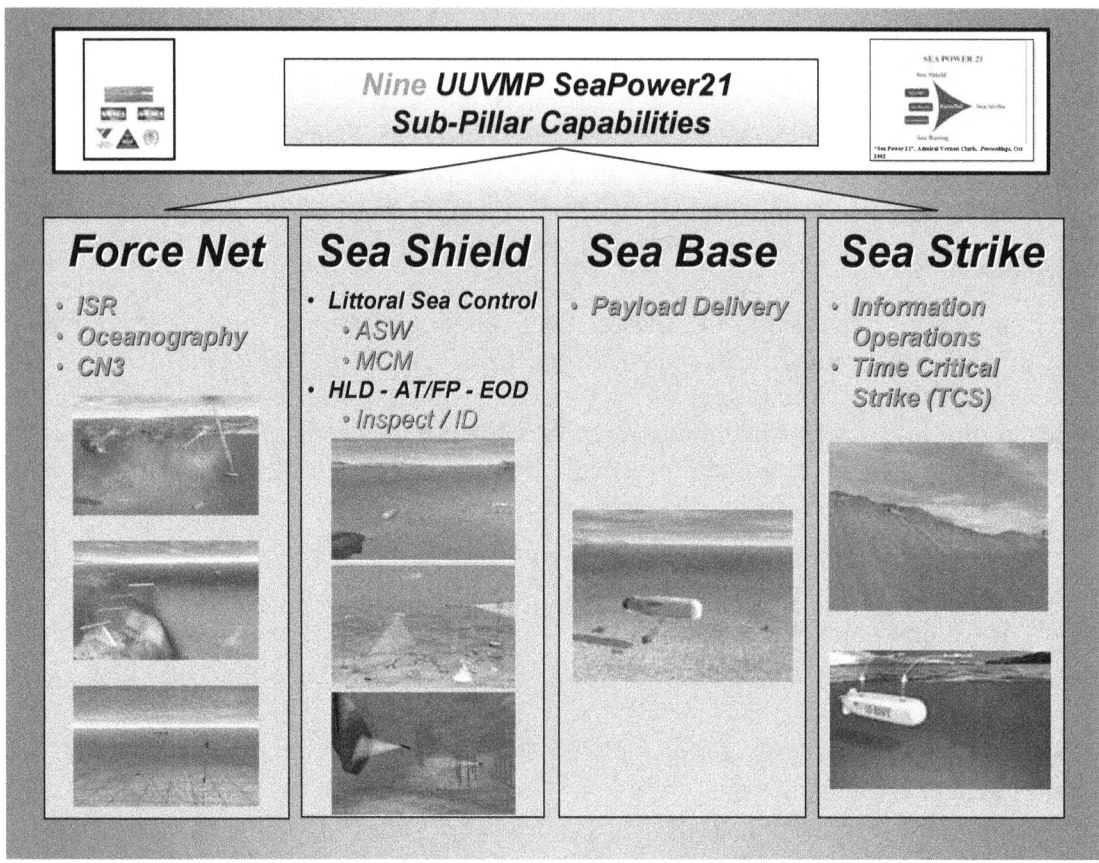

Figure ES-3. Sea Power 21 Sub-Pillar Groupings

FORCEnet

The FORCEnet Pillar encompasses the ISR, Oceanography and Communications / Navigation Network Nodes (CN3) missions; however, its reach crosses all pillars.

Intelligence, Surveillance, and Reconnaissance (ISR): The ISR capability will complement and expand existing capabilities, extending the reach into denied areas, and enabling missions in water too shallow or otherwise inaccessible for conventional platforms. This capability will include multi-function systems, operating from a variety of platforms, enabling the collection of critical electromagnetic and electro-optic data.

Oceanography: This capability provides for the collection of hydrographic and oceanographic data in all ocean environments. Ocean survey supports real-time operations as well as intelligence preparation of the battlespace (IPB) for expected operations. Oceanographic data and environmental products are provided in near real-time for tactical support, archived for long-term support, and provided in rapid-turnaround mode for operational battlespace preparation.

Communication / Navigation Network Nodes (CN3): This capability will be an enabling undersea component of FORCEnet. CN3 systems will provide connectivity across multiple platforms, both manned and unmanned, as well as navigation assistance on demand. Communication and navigation modules developed as part of this capability will transition into other UUV systems, reducing the overall developmental burden and risk.

SEA SHIELD

The Sea Shield Pillar encompasses the Mine Countermeasures, Anti-Submarine Warfare, and Homeland Defense Inspection / Identification missions.

Mine Countermeasures (MCM): The objective of this capability is to find or create Fleet Operating Areas that are clear of sea mines without requiring manned platforms to enter potentially mined areas and to accelerate the MCM timelines. This capability is to operate within the near-term Navy force structure and not adversely impact other warfighting capabilities. It is to provide the least complex and most cost effective solution to the widest range of requirements. The vision is to field a common set of unmanned, modular MCM systems employable from a variety of host platforms or shore sites that can quickly counter the spectrum of mines to enable assured access with minimum risk from mines.

Anti-Submarine Warfare (ASW): This capability focuses on the Task Force ASW "Hold at Risk" scenario, in which a UUV, aided by third-party cueing, monitors and tracks adversary submarine traffic during port egress or through other choke points. The objective of this capability is to patrol, detect, track, and hand off adversary submarines to U.S. Forces using UUVs. A further objective is to perform this function under any rules of engagement and without taking actions that could inadvertently escalate the conflict. Given the potential access restrictions due to bathymetry or enemy forces, the likelihood that undersea forces may be the only forces available early in the conflict, and the desire to track submarines regardless of the stage of hostilities, the UUV is a leading candidate for the "Hold at Risk" task.

Inspection / Identification: The Inspection / Identification capability will support Homeland Defense (HLD), Anti-Terrorism / Force Protection (AT/FP), and Explosive Ordnance Disposal (EOD) needs. It will be able to perform a rapid search function with object investigation and localization in confined areas such as ship hulls, in and around pier pilings, and the bottoms of berthing areas. As stated in the *Explosive Ordnance Disposal (EOD) Anti-Terrorism / Force Protection (AT/FP) Unmanned Underwater Vehicle (UUV) Mission Requirement Priorities,* the goal is to be able to "rapidly reconnoiter areas of concern (e.g., hulls, port areas, and other underwater areas) and to detect, investigate and localize unexploded ordnance (UXO) objects that impose a threat to military forces, high value assets navigable waterways and homeland security."

SEA BASE

The Sea Base pillar encompasses the Payload Delivery Sub-Pillar Capability.

Payload Delivery: The objective of the Payload Delivery capability is to provide a clandestine method of delivering logistics to support a variety of other mission areas. The missions supported include MCM, CN3, ASW, Oceanography, Special Operations Forces Support, and Time Critical Strike (TCS).

SEA STRIKE

The Sea Strike pillar encompasses the Information Operations (IO) and Time Critical Strike (TCS) Sub-Pillar capabilities.

Information Operations (IO): The objective of Information Operations is to "exploit, deceive, deter and disrupt our enemies." These operations can use virtually any platform, weapon or means. The UUV capability to operate clandestinely in shallow waters and areas too hazardous for a manned platform make them ideally suited for several IO missions that could not be performed by other platforms. The two IO roles that UUVs seem best suited for are employment as a submarine decoy and use as a communications or computer node jammer.

Time Critical Strike (TCS): This is in the Kinetic Effects portion of the Sea Strike pillar of Sea Power 21. TCS provides the capability to deliver ordnance to a target with sensor-to-shooter closure measured in seconds, rather than minutes or hours. These operations can use virtually any platform, vehicle, or weapon within the battlespace. Launching a weapon from a UUV, or a UUV delivered weapon cache, allows a launch point closer to the target resulting in quicker response time for prosecution. It also moves the "flaming datum" away from high value platforms so that their positions are not exposed

Recommendations and Conclusions

The overall goal of the UUV Master Plan is to:

Deliver UUV Capability…and Begin Using It!

To accomplish this goal, a number of recommendations are made for the development plan of UUV programs, including the formation of four general vehicle classes, recommendations for technology development, and increased involvement with Fleet experimentation.

The specific recommendations of this Master Plan Update are:

Develop Four Vehicle Classes

Meeting mission requirements and minimizing cost are the two major considerations that must be addressed when developing UUV acquisition programs. To address the nine Sea Power 21 Sub-Pillar capabilities, this document recommends evolving towards four vehicle classes. This will be achieved through integration of current and future UUV programs. In the long term, this evolution will lead to efficiencies in handling systems, other platform interfaces, and interchange of payloads. The four general vehicle classes identified to address the sub-pillar capabilities are:

The Man-Portable class, which includes vehicles from about 25 to 100 pounds displacement, with an endurance of 10 - 20 hours. There is no specific hull shape for this class.

The Light Weight Vehicle (LWV) class, which is nominally 12.75 inches in diameter vehicles and displaces about 500 pounds. Payload increases six- to 12-fold over the man-portable class and endurance is doubled.

The Heavy Weight Vehicle (HWV) class, which is 21 inches in diameter and displaces about 3000 pounds, and provides another factor of two improvement in capability. This class includes submarine compatible vehicles.

The Large Vehicle class will be approximately 10 long-tons displacement and compatible with both surface ship (Littoral Combat Ship (LCS)) and submarine (SSNs with hanger or "plug," and SSGN) use.

The applicability of the four classes of vehicles to the Sea Power 21 Sub-Pillars is shown in Figure ES-4.

Seapower Pillar	Priority	Sub Pillar Capability	Man Portable	LWV	HWV	Large
FORCEnet	1	Intelligence, Surveillance, Reconnaissance	Special Purpose	Harbor	Tactical	Persistent
FORCEnet	5	Oceanography		Special Purpose	Littoral Access	Long Range
FORCEnet	6	Communication / Navigation Network Nodes	VSW / SOF	Mobile CN3		
Sea Shield	2	Mine Countermeasures	VSW / SW SCM / RI Neutralizers	OPAREA Clearance	Clandestine Recon.	
Sea Shield	3	Anti-Submarine Warfare				Hold-at-Risk
Sea Shield	4	Inspection / ID	HLD/ATFP			
Sea Base	7	Payload Delivery				SOF, ASW, MCM, TCS**
Sea Strike	8	Information Operations		Network Attack	Submarine Decoy	
Sea Strike	9	Time Critical Strike				(see Payload Delivery)

Figure ES-4. General Classes of UUV Sizes vs. Sub-Pillar

Varied configurations or "flavors" are expected within classes. For example, the Man-Portable class includes gliders, hovering vehicles, and Fleet fielded Semi-Autonomous Hydrographic Reconnaissance Vehicle (SAHRV) and SCULPIN systems.

The roadmap of Figure ES-5 illustrates how existing UUV efforts will evolve to four vehicle classes. Some capabilities have already been fielded and others are in the late stages of test and evaluation. Lightweight and large vehicle efforts are advanced in the commercial world, and are being leveraged to serve Fleet requirements.

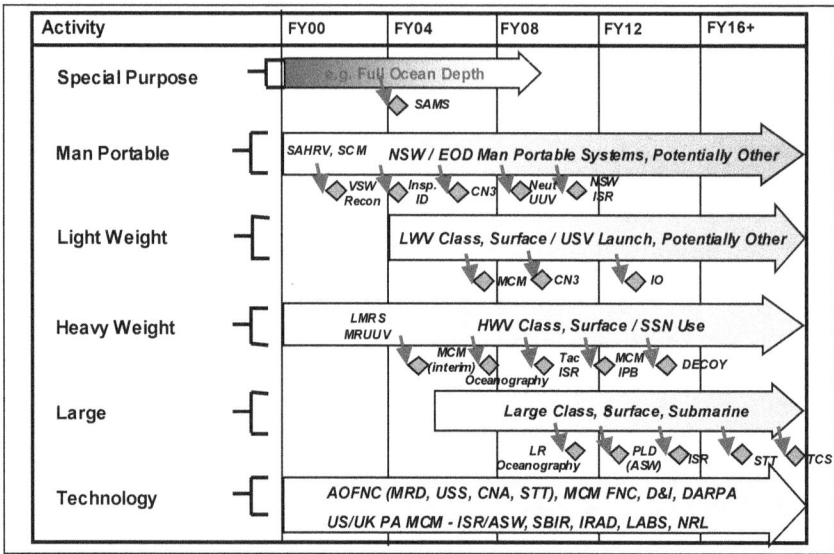

Figure ES-5. UUV Master Plan Program Roadmap

Develop Standards and Implement Modularity

The programmatic recommendation to continue to develop standards for UUVs will ease interchangeability of modules. By developing and following up-to-date standard interfaces, the need for custom interfaces is mitigated or eliminated. Use of Commercial-Off-the-Shelf (COTS) equipment will drive acceptance of current commercial practice and standards. Use of Navy and DoD standards such as FORCEnet based architectures will ensure UUV interoperability with other systems.

Maintain a Balanced UUV Technology Program

A balanced technology program for both UUV payloads and platforms will be maintained. The program should support the nine capabilities described in this document. This study noted the excellent progress of the R&D community in meeting many of the technical recommendations of the last UUV Master Plan. Based on the technical assessment developed in this plan, investment in following critical technologies is recommended:

- Autonomy
- Energy and Propulsion
- Sensors and Sensor Processing
- Communications / Networking
- Engagement / Intervention

Increase Experimentation in UUV Technology

Experimentation with systems should be expanded to provide risk reduction for technology and operations. It is essential to involve Navy operators with outreach to operational, doctrine, and training commands to expand and refine employment concepts. Innovation must be pursued with test and evaluation programs using UUV technologies from government, academia, and industry.

Coordinate with Other Unmanned Vehicle Programs

While there are obvious and distinct differences between requirements for UUVs and other types of unmanned vehicles (e.g., energy, navigation, and communications), there are also numerous areas of commonality (e.g., autonomy and mission planning). Coordination with the developers of the Unmanned Surface Vehicle (USV) and Unmanned Vehicle (UXV) Master Plans, as well as interaction at the technical level, can provide synergies and reduce costs across all the Navy's unmanned vehicle programs.

Field Systems in the Fleet

Continued introduction of functional UUVs into the fleet is critical. Fleet sailors have enthusiastically received a variety of small vehicles since the approval of the last Master Plan. Fleet fielded systems such as SAHRV (Navy Special Warfare-NSW) and SCULPIN (EOD) not only provided operational capabilities in contingencies such as Operation Iraqi Freedom, but also provide a critical pool of educated Fleet UUV operators who are a critical link in the evolution of future generations of UUVs. Execution of larger vehicle programs needs to be in accordance with a "spiral development" philosophy. Some capabilities, even if they are interim, need to be provided to the fleet as soon as possible. *A partial technical solution in-use in the Fleet is worth more than perfection in the laboratory.*

Human Systems Integration (HSI)

The product of UUV use is knowledge and data to the warfighter today, and in the future direct actions that aid the warfighter. As a result, the integration of the unmanned system with the "manned" system is paramount. HSI should be addressed as a major part of every UUV program and exercise.

Conclusion

The goal of the Master Plan is to provide a strategy to rapidly deliver new UUV capabilities to the Fleet, with a strategy for upgrading those capabilities with minimal time and expense. This plan effectively synergizes the efforts under legacy, developmental, and technology programs. Development and fielding of advanced technologies will provide growth and dominance. The establishment of standards will be critical to the success of future systems, for without them the required modularity will not be achieved. The effective introduction of UUVs into the Fleet will significantly contribute to the Navy's control of the maritime battlespace.

Deliver UUV Capability...and Begin Using It!

1   The Vision

Today our naval forces enjoy maritime superiority around the world and find themselves at a strategic inflection point during which future capabilities must be pondered with creativity and innovation. Change must be embraced and made an ally in order to take advantage of emerging technologies, concepts, and doctrine; thereby preserving the nation's global leadership. Sea Power 21 has additionally specified unmanned vehicles as force multipliers and risk reduction agents for the Navy of the future. Transformation applies to *what* we buy as well as *how* we buy and operate it–all while competing with other shifting national investment priorities.

The long-term UUV vision is to have the capability to: (1) deploy or retrieve devices, (2) gather, transmit, or act on all types of information, and (3) engage bottom, volume, surface, air or land targets (See Figure 1-1). The growing use of unmanned systems–air, surface, ground, and underwater is continually demonstrating new possibilities. One can conceive of scenarios where UUVs sense, track, identify, target, and destroy an enemy– all autonomously and tie in with the full net-centric battlespace. UUV systems will provide a key undersea component for FORCEnet, contributing to an integrated picture of the battlespace. Admittedly this vision is futuristic.

Even though today's planners, operators, and technologists cannot accurately forecast the key applications for UUVs in the year 2050, this plan provides a roadmap to move toward that vision. Pursuit of this plan's updated recommendations beginning in the year 2004, will place increasingly large numbers of UUVs in the hands of warfighters. Thus, UUVs can begin addressing near-term needs while improving understanding of mid- to far-term possibilities. Even the most futuristic applications can evolve in a confident, cost-effective manner. This confidence is based on several factors: the Sea Power 21 Sub-Pillar capabilities identified here address a broad range of user needs; critical technologies are identified that will enable tomorrow's more complex applications; and key principles and best practices are recommended that provide for a logical, flexible, and affordable development effort.

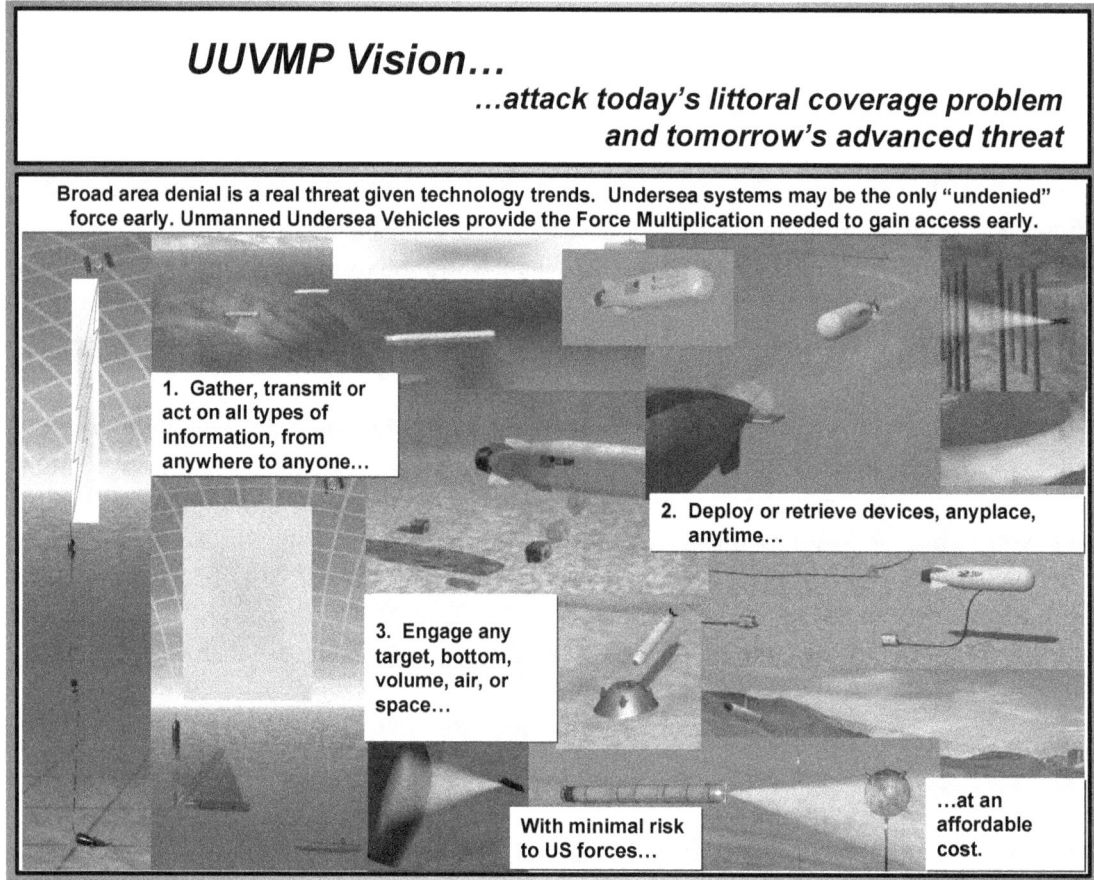

UUVMP Vision...

...attack today's littoral coverage problem and tomorrow's advanced threat

Broad area denial is a real threat given technology trends. Undersea systems may be the only "undenied" force early. Unmanned Undersea Vehicles provide the Force Multiplication needed to gain access early.

1. Gather, transmit or act on all types of information, from anywhere to anyone...

2. Deploy or retrieve devices, anyplace, anytime...

3. Engage any target, bottom, volume, air, or space...

With minimal risk to US forces...

...at an affordable cost.

Figure 1-1. UUV Master Plan Vision

1.1   Navy Needs

The needs of naval forces are briefly reviewed here before discussing how UUVs can support those needs.   Additional refinement of Fleet needs will result from experimentation efforts and feedback from combat operations. For example, UUVs have been involved in combat and support operations in Operation Iraqi Freedom, providing an extension of existing underwater sensing and detection capabilities and a reduced diver workload.

The Navy needs stealthy and unmanned systems to gather information and engage targets in areas denied to traditional maritime forces. Offboard-unmanned systems also need to be considered to improve performance, reduce costs, and expedite tactical mission timelines for Intelligence Preparation of the Battlespace (IPB) and related non-combatant naval activities.   Area denial will increase in both likelihood and extent through the adversary's strategy of asymmetric warfare (the use of easily acquired weapons in innovative ways to exploit our weaknesses, rather than competing head-to-head). Access denial weapons that challenge our forces include quiet submarines, mines, tactical ballistic missiles, cruise missiles, weapons of mass destruction, and information warfare. Space-based surveillance systems, long-range precision strike weapons, and robust command and control networks may also be used by adversaries to further threaten a U.S. Navy whose doctrine and force structure postulate access to the littorals to enable power projection ashore. In addition to direct threats, diplomatic constraints or rules of engagement may preclude the early entry of overt maritime forces. For example, coalition aircraft and ships remained south of a specified latitude during Operation Desert Shield in order to avoid prematurely touching off the ground war. Tools are needed that avoid detection and are resistant to attack, which allow penetration of denied areas for sustained independent operations. In this way military commanders can keep other forces out of harm's way during the initial phases of a conflict while still being able to prepare and shape the battlespace, ensuring ultimate defeat of the area denial threat.

1.2 Sea Power 21 Impact

Sea Power 21 provides overarching guidance for the development and employment of all Navy systems. This plan addresses how UUVs will support the four Sea Power 21 fundamental qualities of:

Decisiveness: Every element of the Navy-Marine Corps Team will be equipped, organized, and trained to bring decisive effects both lethal and non-lethal to bear where it counts.

Sustainability: We are capable of arriving quickly and remaining on scene for extended periods of time. Transforming to fuller sea base capabilities will provide even greater expeditionary capabilities across the naval and joint force.

Responsiveness: Naval forces operate around the world, around the clock, continuing to operate from the sea, free from basing or permission constraints.

Agility: Our forces are creatively packaged. Continuous organizational transformation will create an even more flexible and responsive Force.

The missions defined in this document will be classified in terms of the Sea Power 21 "…three fundamental concepts: Sea Strike, Sea Shield, and Sea Base, enabled by FORCEnet."

Sea Strike is a broadened concept for naval power projection that leverages enhanced Command, Control, Communications, Computers, Intelligence, Surveillance, and Reconnaissance (C4ISR), precision, stealth, and endurance to increase operational tempo, reach, and effectiveness.

Sea Shield develops naval capabilities related to homeland defense, sea control, assured access, and projecting defense overland. By doing so, it reassures allies, strengthens deterrence, and protects the joint force.

Sea Base projects the sovereignty of the United States globally while providing Joint Force Commanders with vital command and control, fire support, and logistics from the sea, thereby minimizing vulnerable assets ashore.

FORCEnet is the operational construct and architectural framework for naval warfare in the Information age, which integrates warriors, sensors, networks, command and control, platforms and weapons into a networked, distributed combat force.

1.3   UUV Possibilities

Sea Power 21 also directs that the Navy will "Use unmanned platforms: Air, Land, Sea, and Undersea for combat and reconnaissance," as well as postulates a host of specific missions (e. g., mine warfare, shallow-water anti-submarine warfare (ASW)) for which UUVs are uniquely suited. Current and future UUV development should continue to focus on facilitating the Navy's high-priority missions.

Creative thought about and planning for the future of UUVs and their naval applications is still required. An "unmanned undersea vehicle" is defined as a:

Self-propelled submersible whose operation is either fully autonomous (pre-programmed or real-time adaptive mission control) or under minimal supervisory control and is untethered except, possibly, for data links such as a fiber optic cable.

This document does not address towed systems, hard-tethered devices such as remotely operated vehicles, systems not capable of fully submerging such as Unmanned Surface Vehicles (USV), semi-submersible vehicles, or bottom crawlers.

While their inherent characteristics make them more clearly suited for some applications than others, UUVs can offer capabilities in each of these areas, particularly in preparation of the battlespace in the face of area denial threats that may present undue risks to manned systems. The many possibilities for UUVs to contribute to naval needs derive from their operational advantages, which include:

Autonomy. The ability to operate independently for extended periods creates a force multiplier that allows manned systems to extend their reach and focus on more complex tasks. Costs may be reduced when sensors or weapons are operated from the smaller infrastructure of a UUV rather than entirely from manned platforms.

Risk Reduction. Their unmanned nature lessens or eliminates risk to personnel from the environment, the enemy, and the unforgiving sea.

Low Profile. UUVs operate fully submerged with potentially low acoustic and electromagnetic signatures. They maintain a low profile when surfaced to extend antennae. The possible intent for follow-on manned operations in a route or area is not revealed and the element of surprise is preserved. UUVs have less risk of entanglement with underwater or floating obstructions than towed or hard-tethered systems (remotely operated vehicles (ROVs)).

Deployability. By virtue of their potentially smaller size, UUVs can provide a capability organic to the strike group. They can also be designed as "flyaway" packages or be pre-positioned in forward areas. Their launch can be adapted to a variety of platforms including ships, submarines, aircraft, and shore facilities. The UUV recovery craft need not be the same as the launch craft. Recovery may be delayed or dismissed entirely for low-cost expendable systems. Multiple UUVs can be deployed simultaneously from one platform.

Environmental Adaptability. UUVs can operate in all water depths, in foul weather and seas, under tropical or arctic conditions, and around the clock. Their ability to operate in the medium gives them unique sensor advantages over similar towed or surface operated sensors.

Persistence. UUVs can remain on station in the face of weather that would abort the operations of an Unmanned Aerial Vehicle (UAV) or USV, simply by submerging to a calmer depth. Violent weather may preclude near-surface operations, but UUVs can wait out the storm at depth, precluding a lengthy transit when conditions improve. Likewise, UUVs that lose power (accidentally or intentionally in a "loiter" mode) can settle stably onto the bottom, unlike UAVs and USVs that are at the mercy of the elements as soon as they lose propulsion.

UUVs should be used in applications where they increase performance, lower cost, enable missions that cannot be performed by manned systems, or reduce the risk to manned systems. The characteristics of UUVs that may facilitate meeting these principles include their ability to put sensors in an optimal position in both the vertical and horizontal dimensions, autonomy, endurance, low-observability, expendability, and standoff or reach from the launch platform.

1.4   Linkage to Other UUV Plans and Studies

This document is consistent with and amplifies the challenges of the April 2000 UUV Master Plan (UUVMP), its predecessors, and successors:

- 1994: Navy UUV Program Plan (N87)–focused on immediate needs for clandestine mine reconnaissance from submarines (Near-Term Mine Reconnaissance System (NMRS) first priority, Long-Term Mine Reconnaissance System (LMRS) second priority and Tactical Oceanography third priority) with minor updates in 1995 and 1997

- April 2000: UUV Master Plan (ASN/RDA) – future focus, other missions and users

- June 2002: Small UUV Strategic Plan (PEO MUW) – Linked to UUVMP, added detail for Explosive Ordnance Disposal (EOD), Very Shallow Water (VSW) Mine Countermeasures (MCM) and Shallow-water MCM

Significant portions of the 2000 plan are now well on the way to completion. Although the 2000 plan did not espouse any particular program or technical implementation, the Navy and other developers have made strides toward making all four of the former signature capabilities a reality.

Since 2000, additional studies have been performed that provide guidance. This guidance included assessments not only of the role of UUVs, but also of the operational effectiveness of various sizes and configurations of UUVs in missions of high interest to the Navy. Those plans and studies include the studies associated with the 21-inch Mission Reconfigurable UUV, the Analysis of Alternatives (AoA) for the Large Displacement UUVs and for the Explosive Ordnance Disposal UUVs, the SSGN Sensors and Payloads Study, and several Naval War College and Navy Warfare Development Command studies and war games. A complete listing of documents referenced is provided in Appendix A. This UUV Master Plan Update builds on the 2000 UUV Master Plan, updating the missions, approaches, and technical and programmatic recommendations based on changes in Navy guidance, technology, employment platforms, and other factors since April 2000.

2 Missions

In the future, UUVs will perform a myriad of missions supporting Fleet objectives both in wartime and peacetime. The first stage in updating the Master Plan was to generate a comprehensive pool of potential UUV missions. During this stage the goal was to develop a wide-ranging innovative list of potential UUV applications without regard to technical feasibility, political acceptability, or affordability. The missions generated were then analyzed and prioritized in accordance with Fleet and national needs.

2.1 Mission Generation Methodology

A wide variety of mission sources were sought, including a broad range of current and potential UUV users. The UUV Master Plan Study Team accomplished this through field surveys, expert panel discussions, workshops, examination of the literature, and analysis.

2.1.1 UUV Master Plan Study Team

The Study Team developing the original plan consisted of UUV experts from a wide range of Navy laboratories and academia. These team members had extensive experience in UUV applications for mine countermeasures, anti-submarine warfare, search and salvage, deep ocean object recovery, military oceanography, surveillance, inspection, and undersea work (Appendix C). A similar set of UUV experts was assembled for the Master Plan Update (Appendix D). Several members served both studies. In addition, UUV resource sponsors and fleet users of systems served on the update team.

2.1.2 Year 2000 Field Surveys and Expert Panels

For the year 2000 Master Plan, interviews were performed with a large number of potential users in the Fleet, industry, science and academia, and other federal agencies (Appendix B). Emphasis was placed on potential users of UUVs as opposed to those solely involved with technology development. A broad cross-section of interviewers and interviewees spanned the full range of UUV applications. An additional group of visionary experts in the underwater field was brought together for an innovation workshop to bring forward ideas and inventive concepts for UUV application and development.

The users surveyed expressed both unique and overlapping UUV mission needs. High priority missions included Intelligence, Surveillance, and Reconnaissance (ISR); Mine Countermeasures (MCM); Anti-Submarine Warfare (ASW); and Oceanography. Industry is pursuing UUV applications for long-range cable and pipelaying surveys and for subsea intervention and operations. Scientific applications included detailed bathymetric mapping, deep-water sampling, and use as a long-term observation platform. Other government agencies also expressed the need for UUVs in hazardous waste operations, fisheries research, drug interdiction, and bathymetric mapping.

2.1.3 Update Study Workshops

For the UUVMP update in 2004, a series of three workshops was held to gather inputs from Navy UUV operators, stakeholders, Navy laboratories, academia, and industry

(Figure 2.1). The primary goal of the first workshop was to collect operational perspectives and mission needs from the Fleet, and to further evaluate potential applications for UUVs. A list of potential UUV missions was gathered and prioritized. The second and third workshops refined this list of missions and developed a Navy strategy for using UUVs to meet its expected operational needs. A more detailed description of the three workshops is provided in Appendix E.

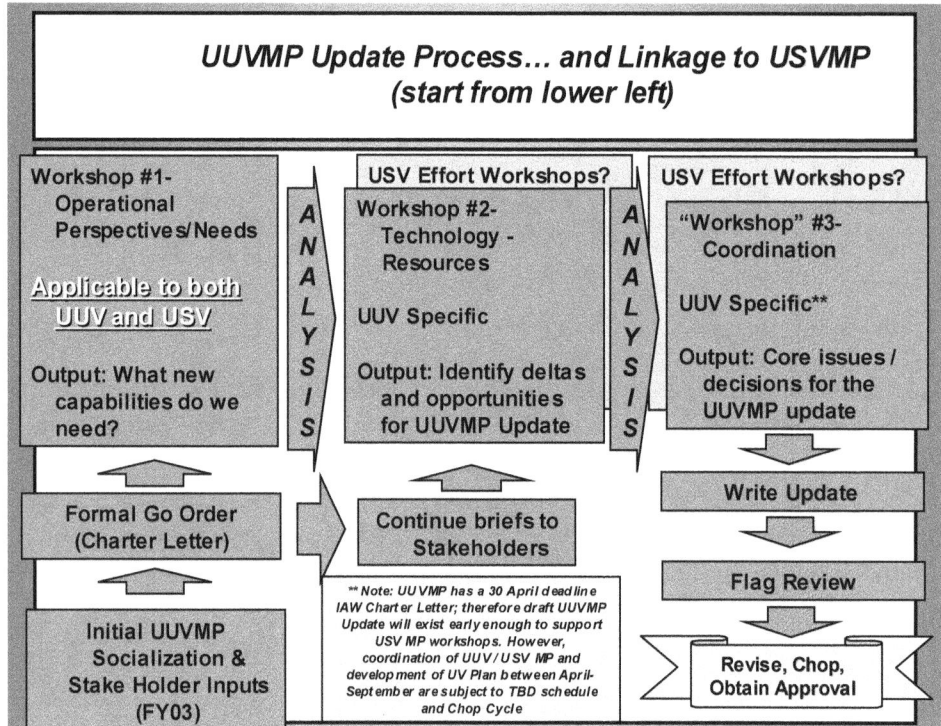

Figure 2-1. UUVMP Update Workshop Process Flow

2.1.4 Related Studies

In addition to the field studies, panel discussions, and workshops, the Study Team reviewed existing UUV applications and technologies literature. A number of studies have been performed examining the various roles and status of UUV systems and technologies.

For the year 2000 Master Plan, key documents included the 1996 National Research Council Report *Undersea Vehicles and National Needs* and the 1999 Marine Technology Society CD-ROM *Operational Effectiveness of Unmanned Underwater Systems.* Relevant conference proceedings, including the *IEEE / MTS OCEANS, ADC / MTS Underwater Intervention, U.S. Naval Mine Countermeasures Plan,* and *Unmanned Undersea Submersible Technology,* were surveyed to ascertain the state of the art in academic and commercial UUV development.

For the UUV Master Plan update, documents surveyed included the *Sea Power 21, Naval Transformation Roadmap,* the *FORCEnet Architecture and Standards, November 2003,* the Naval Research Advisory Committee (NRAC) report *Roles of Unmanned Vehicles, March 2002,* and the *Navy Strategic Plan for Small Unmanned Underwater Vehicles, June 2002.* Additional studies referenced included the Office of Naval Research's

(ONR's) *Contested Submarine Mission Area/Concept of Operations (CONOPS) Study*, the *Organic Mine Countermeasures End-to-End Assessment*, and the Naval War College's study of *Roles and Missions for UUVs*. All information gathered was incorporated in the mission generation and analysis for the plan.

2.1.5 Study Team Analysis

Once the list of missions was generated, the Study Team analyzed the data, looking for the common and high priority mission characteristics. Key evaluation criteria included mission type, degree of innovation, uniqueness of the UUV ability, technology development required, multiple applications, and overall importance to the Navy. This analysis resulted in the generation of key mission categories and the prioritization of missions to be pursued, as discussed in the sections below.

2.2 Mission Categories

Mission analysis for both the original UUVMP and this Update fell into several general categories: ISR; MCM; ASW; Oceanography; Communication / Navigation Network Nodes (CN3, called "Communication / Navigation Aid" in the original plan); Inspection / Identification; Payload Delivery; Information Operations (IO); Time Critical Strike (TCS); Barrier Patrol; and Sea-Base Support. Each of these categories addresses key Navy needs and has its own set of mission characteristics and requirements. All of the missions generated, from the simplest to the futuristic, are discussed below.

2.2.1 Intelligence, Surveillance and Reconnaissance (ISR)

Persistent ISR is an identified Navy need. ISR is important not only for the traditional purpose of intelligence collection, but also as a precursor and enabler for other missions, such as MCM and ASW. The ISR mission area encompasses collection and delivery of many types of data: intelligence collection of all types, target detection and localization, and mapping (e.g. IPB and Oceanography). UUVs are uniquely suited for information collection due to their ability to operate at long standoff distances, operate in shallow water areas, operate autonomously, and provide a level of clandestine capability not available with other systems. UUVs extend the reach of their host platforms into inaccessible or contested areas. UUVs also act as a force multiplier by increasing the number of sensors in the battlespace. There are many applications, particularly of a military nature, where UUVs would be the preferred means of persistently and clandestinely gathering desired information. UUVs can operate in otherwise denied areas, and provide information without undue risk to personnel or high value assets. Possible ISR UUV missions include:

- Persistent and tactical intelligence collection: Signal, Electronic, Measurement, and Imaging Intelligence (SIGINT, ELINT, MASINT, and IMINT), Meteorology and Oceanography (METOC), etc. (above and/or below ocean surface)
- Chemical, Biological, Nuclear, Radiological, and Explosive (CBNRE) detection and localization (both above and below the ocean surface)
- Near-Land and Harbor Monitoring
- Deployment of leave-behind surveillance sensors or sensor arrays
- Specialized mapping and object detection and localization

2.2.2   Mine Countermeasures (MCM)

MCM mission requirements are driven by the Fleet's need to rapidly establish large, safe operating areas and transit routes (Q-routes) and lanes. These areas are typified by long sea-lines of communication (SLOCs), offshore Fleet Operating Areas (e.g., Carrier Operating Areas (COAs), Amphibious Operating Areas (AOAs)), and Littoral Penetration Areas (e.g., Assault Breach, Port Break-in, STOM) as depicted in Figure 2-1. These range in size from 100 to 900 Nmi^2 or larger, and cover the water column from deep, mineable waters to on the beach in support of Marine Corps operations as seen in Figure 2-3. While it is desirable to minimize risk to the Fleet operating in these areas, time is paramount. Seven to ten days is emerging as the requirement to complete all MCM operations in these areas, but clearly, quicker is better. These operations need to be completed before the bulk of the Fleet arrives in the area. Therefore, lift, control, and replenishment of MCM assets are key considerations in the Concept of Operations (CONOPS).

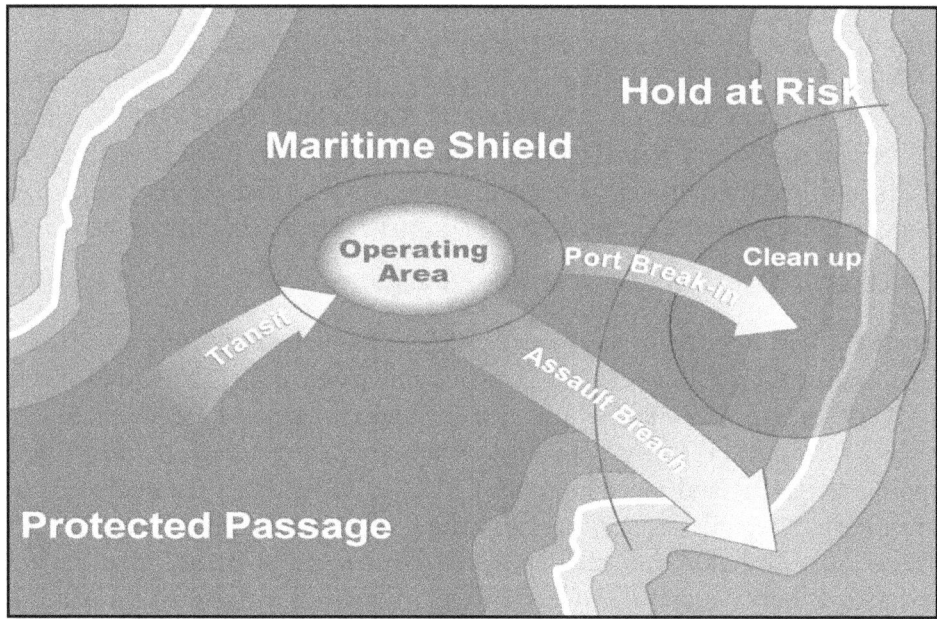

Figure 2-2. MIW Mission Areas

10

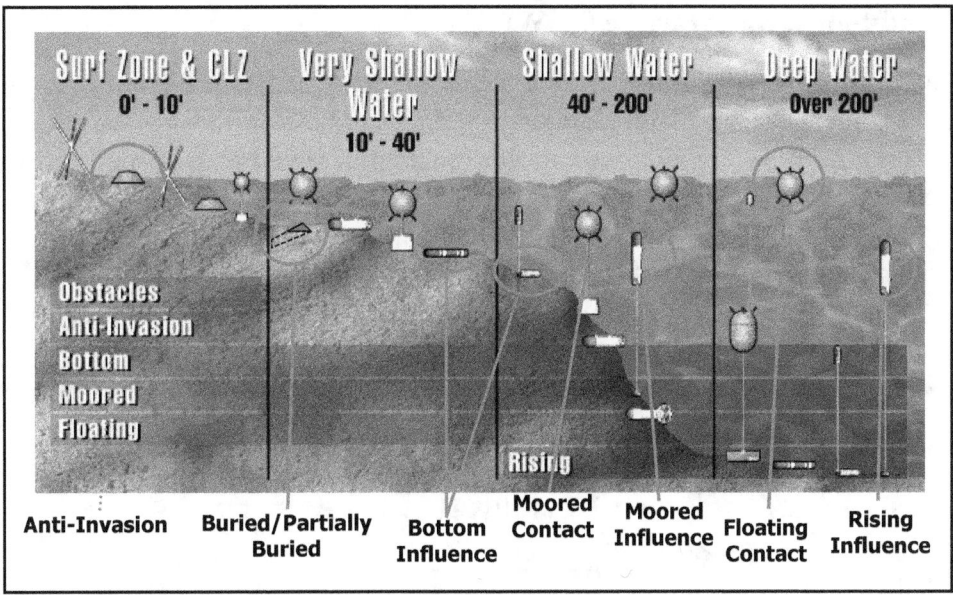

Figure 2-3. Littoral Mine Threats

In general, the overt nature of conventional MCM operations becomes more of a concern closer to shore. Large area operations, far out at sea, do not signal the Fleet's intent as clearly as near-shore operations. It is becoming clear that operational deception (i.e., a tactic that appears to spread operations over so large a front that the actual objective cannot be discerned) may frequently be as effective as totally clandestine operations. This may relax some engineering and cost constraints. However, in some cases, clandestine MCM remains a requirement.

The full range of MCM mission types can be brought to bear to meet these requirements against the myriad mine threat types and operational environments. These include:
- Reconnaissance—Detection, classification, identification and localization.
- Clearance—Neutralization and breaching.
- Sweeping—Mechanical and influence.
- Protection—Spoofing and jamming.

Additionally, other mission areas contribute to MCM operations. For example, IPB can be accomplished with a variety of ISR assets. These assets can indicate if mine stockpiles have been accessed, mines moved, minelayers loaded, or mining operations undertaken, thereby allowing actions against these threats prior to their deployment. UUVs can gather oceanographic data long before hostile operations to provide data on winds, bathymetry, water visibility, currents, waves, bottom geophysical parameters, kelp concentrations, sand bars, etc. to determine mineable areas. Previous bottom surveys can be compared to current ones to determine changes in mine-like contacts.

2.2.3 Anti-Submarine Warfare (ASW)

Task Force ASW has instituted a new focus on, and understanding of littoral ASW operations. Figure 2-4 shows the categories, which can be described as:
- "Hold at Risk"–monitoring all the submarines that exit a port or transit a chokepoint.
- "Maritime Shield"–clearing and maintaining a large Carrier or Expeditionary Strike Group (CSG or ESG) operating area free of threat submarines.
- "Protected Passage"–clearing and maintaining a route for an ESG from one operating area to another free of threat submarines.

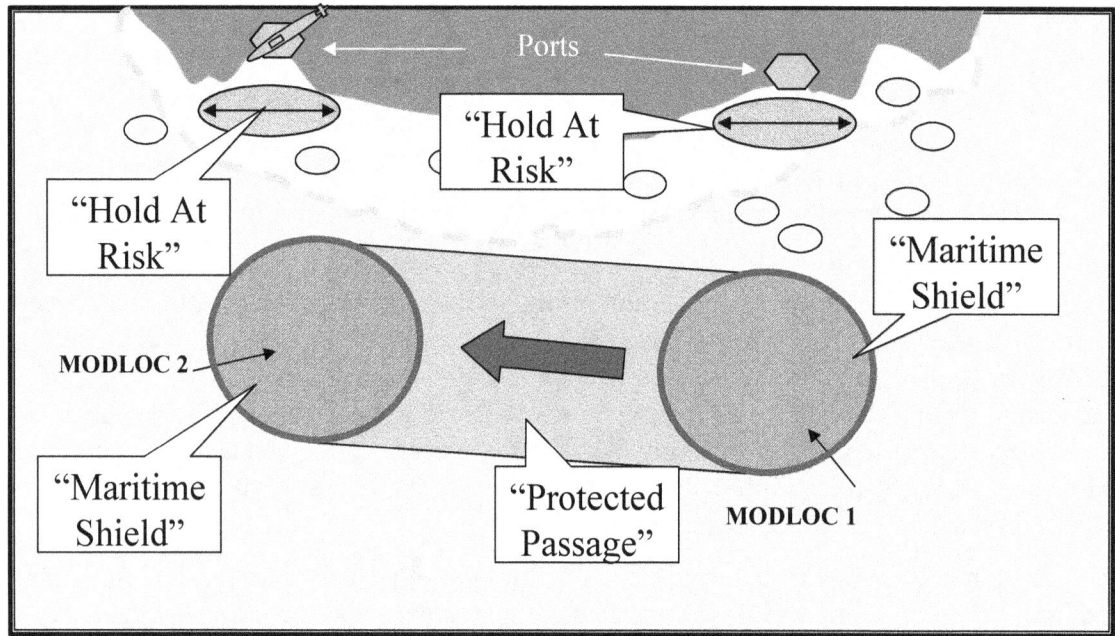

Figure 2-4. Task Force ASW Nomenclature

UUVs offer significant force multiplication for ASW operations in the Hold at Risk scenario. While offering some advantages in the other two categories, the UUVs limited mobility and the lesser need for stealth make UUVs less ideal candidates in those cases. In all cases, UUVs can serve as offboard sensors or sources, extending the range of detection without increasing risk. The host platform can serve as the mother ship for a fleet of vehicles, providing the decision-making capabilities while remaining out of harm's way.

In the Hold at Risk scenario, UUVs can provide major force multiplication for existing ASW forces. By establishing submarine surveillance points without escalating the level of conflict, UUVs in the Hold at Risk scenario can greatly enhance the ability of the Task Force Commander to achieve and maintain access, independent of the state of hostilities. In addition to using existing or pre-positioned sensor fields and cueing assets, the UUV may also be tasked to plant its own field (a sub-mission which falls under the category of Payload Delivery).

Variations on the Hold at Risk mission, depending on the stage of conflict and the implementation of appropriate CONOPs and Rules of Engagement (ROE), include: (a)

UUV employment of non-lethal weaponry, (b) employment of lethal weaponry, and (c) accumulation of intelligence information on threat submarines, individually and collectively.

2.2.4   Inspection / Identification (ID)

Among the many requirements emerging from Homeland Defense (HLD) and Anti-Terrorism / Force Protection (AT/FP) is the need to efficiently inspect ship hulls and piers for foreign objects.   Currently, hull and pier inspection is generally the responsibility of EOD Diver teams, and it is both time and manpower intensive.   The demand for security swims around piers and hulls has resulted in over a six-fold increase in these diver operations since the events of September 11, 2001 (*Navy Safety Center Diver Data Base)*.   Additional assets beyond the available EOD Diver teams are needed to effectively meet these additional requirements for inspection.

The typical targets in a hull or pier search would be unexploded ordnance, such as limpet mines or special attack charges.   Critical components of the ship such as shafts, intakes and discharges must be secured before a diver can begin his search.   Preparing a ship for divers may take several hours, and it requires coordination, as some damage control systems may have to remain on-line.   Searching for ordnance that is typically time-fused is particularly hazardous to divers.   Use of an unmanned vehicle can reduce the risk to EOD technicians and divers by providing precise location of suspicious objects, while relieving the divers of the tedious search process in cluttered environments.

2.2.5   Oceanography

Knowledge of the operating environment is of key importance for both strategic and tactical operations. UUVs are well suited for many ocean survey tasks.   Conventional oceanographic data collection is largely dependent on hull mounted or towed systems that require extensive surface ship support and suffer limitations imposed by tow cables. In applications such as acoustic and optical imaging, data quality is significantly enhanced when sensors are decoupled from motion of a towing platform.

UUVs permit characterization of significantly greater areas at less cost by multiplying the effectiveness of existing platforms.   UUVs can perform oceanographic reconnaissance in near-shore shallow water areas while their host ships remain at a safe standoff range. UUV technology provides the opportunity to acquire affordable, near real-time data at required temporal and spatial sampling densities.   Data gathered by UUVs will be integrated with conventional survey data and models to provide joint warfighters with critical knowledge of the undersea battlespace. UUVs can autonomously collect information for later delivery and analysis for battlespace preparation or for direct transmission and real-time input into Tactical Decision Aids (TDAs).

Oceanography missions for UUV operations include:
- Bottom Mapping
    - Bathymetry
    - Acoustic imagery
    - Optical imagery
    - Subbottom profiling
    - Water column characterization

- Ocean current profiles (with tides)
  o Temperature profiles
  o Salinity profiles
  o Water clarity
  o Bioluminescence
  o CBN detection and tracking

These missions support safety at sea and all naval warfare areas.

2.2.6 Communications / Navigation Network Node (CN3)

UUVs can serve as critical communication and navigation links between various platforms–at sea, on shore, even into the air and space realms. As with the other missions, they can be operated from a variety of platforms, at long standoff distances, and for extended periods of time. A small vehicle can function as an information conduit between a subsea platform and an array, or it can clandestinely come to the surface and provide a discreet antenna. As an aid to navigation, UUVs can serve as stand-by buoys, positioning themselves at designated locations and popping to the surface to provide visual or other references for military maneuvers or other operations. UUVs can also provide the link between subsurface platforms and Global Positioning System (GPS) or other navigation system, without exposing the platform to unnecessary risk. Pre-positioned beacons could be placed to provide navigational references in circumstances where conventional means are not available or desirable for use. This makes them attractive for a variety of communication and navigation functions including the following:

Communication: "Phone booths": underwater network nodes for data transmission
Underwater connectors (e.g., "Flying Plug")
Low aspect deployed antennas (SATCOM, GPS)

Navigation: Deployment of transponders or mobile transponders
Inverted GPS capability (antenna to surface)
On-demand channel lane markers (to support Amphibious Assault)

2.2.7 Payload Delivery

Large UUVs can facilitate logistics by providing clandestine supply and support without exposing high-value platforms. Potential payloads include:

- Supplies to preposition for Special Operations Force (SOF) or EOD missions.
- Cargo as a follow on behind SEAL Delivery Vehicles (SDVs)
- Sensors or vehicles deployed in support of ISR, ASW, Mine Warfare (MIW), Oceanography, CN3 or Time Critical Strike (TCS)
- MCM neutralization devices
- Weapons to deploy or preposition

2.2.8 Information Operations (IO)

Analysis by the study group identified two IO roles well suited to UUVs: First, as a platform to jam or inject false data into enemy communications or computer networks, and second, as submarine decoy.

The small size and stealth inherent in UUVs would enable them to operate in coastal areas difficult or impossible for other platforms, where they could carry antennas and transmitters into locations that support electronic attack. The degree of difficulty increases as the capability moves from jamming to denial of services to injection of false data.

Submarine decoys and ASW training targets have existed for decades. These simple vehicles could be effectively used in an IO role to convince an enemy that submarines are operating in an area where they, in fact, are not. Today's capabilities could improve on this old technology by extending the range, duration and autonomy of the vehicles to provide an improved deception capability. This capability could be used to impede enemy maritime operations out of fear of attack by a non-existent or minimal submarine threat. In addition, they would enhance the safety of friendly submarines by causing the enemy to dilute its ASW forces into areas where friendly submarines are not operating.

2.2.9   Time Critical Strike (TCS)

Warfighters need the ability to strike time critical targets at precisely the right moment in battle. UUVs can perform some of the necessary functions for TCS, for example, clandestine weapon delivery or remote launch. Stealth and long-standoff distance and duration allow a UUV to be an effective weapon platform or weapon cache delivery vehicle for TCS missions. Launching a weapon from a UUV or from an emplaced cache allows a launch point closer to the target resulting in reduced fuel weight requirements and quicker response time for prosecution. It also moves the "flaming datum" away from high value platforms so that their positions are not exposed. The autonomous weapon or weapon launch option is controversial, however weapon launch from an unmanned vehicle has been accomplished in wartime conditions, specifically from the Predator UAV. Man-in-the-loop control of weapon launch will be required for the foreseeable future.

2.2.10 Barrier Patrol for Homeland Defense and Force Protection

UUVs could perform a barrier patrol in and around harbors to search for undersea threats to ships, piers, and harbor infrastructure. These threats can include manned and unmanned underwater vehicles, swimmers, and remotely deployed mines. Using unmanned vehicles to perform these barrier patrols can save cost by reducing the number of personnel needed to patrol harbors. While there is no need to perform the homeland defense mission clandestinely, in some cases it may be beneficial to place the vehicle and sensor underwater with the threat.

2.2.11 Sea Base Support

UUVs could perform a barrier patrol for an Expeditionary or Carrier Strike Group by operating ahead of the strike group and performing a search for submerged threats. However, this mission presents a significant technical challenge for UUVs due to the requirements for long endurance and the high speeds required to operate ahead of a strike group.

2.3   Mission Prioritization / Suitability for UUVs

The eleven mission areas discussed in this chapter were prioritized via a combination of assessment of the original plan, voting at individual workshops, and Team analysis. The missions were also assessed in terms of: suitability for UUV application (vs. some other manned or unmanned platform) and the degree to which cross-mission support occurred.

The original plan prioritized the Signature Capabilities, and hence the following five missions, in this order:

- Maritime Reconnaissance (ISR)
- Undersea Search and Survey (MCM)
- Undersea Search and Survey (Oceanography)
- Communication and Navigation Aid (CN3)
- Submarine Tracking (ASW).

At the first two workshops, these five missions remained the top five missions. ASW moved up in priority (to second in one workshop and to fourth in the other). The new missions were ranked consistently below these original missions, with the next most important mission being Inspection / Identification (ID) (for homeland defense and anti-terrorism and force-protection (AT/FP). This was to be expected and is consistent with the priority of the Global War on Terror (GWOT).

Figure 2-5 shows the merged mission priority (a compromise between workshop results and Team analysis) and an assessment of the suitability of these missions for UUV application.

SEAPOWER21 Sub-Pillar Missions	Suitability for UUVs
ISR	H
MCM	H
ASW	H
Inspect / ID	H
Oceanography	H
Comm / Nav Networks	MH
Payload Delivery	M
IO	M
Barrier Patrol (HLD / AT-FP)	L
Barrier Patrol (Sea Base Support)	VL
Time Critical Strike (TCS)	M
High (Green) = Best Performed by a UUV	
Medium (Yellow) = Performed Effectively by UUV and other Platforms	
Low (Red) = Best Performed by other Platforms	
BLENDED COLORS = VALUE IS A FUNCTION OF SIZE OR LEVEL OF PERFORMANCE	

Figure 2-5. Merged UUV Mission Priorities

The conclusion from the Study Team analysis is that neither of the barrier patrol type missions, either for Sea Base support or Homeland Defense / AT/FP purposes, is really suitable for UUVs. These missions either require visible deterrence, in the case of HLD / AT/FP, or require such speed of action or transit speeds, that USVs or UAVs would be more appropriate platforms. As a result, the barrier type missions have been dropped from this plan.

As stated at the beginning of this section, this priority order took into account the degree to which the missions were inter-related, as well as the individual priorities. Figure 2-6 shows the degree to which each mission supports the others. More detail will be provided in Chapter 3.

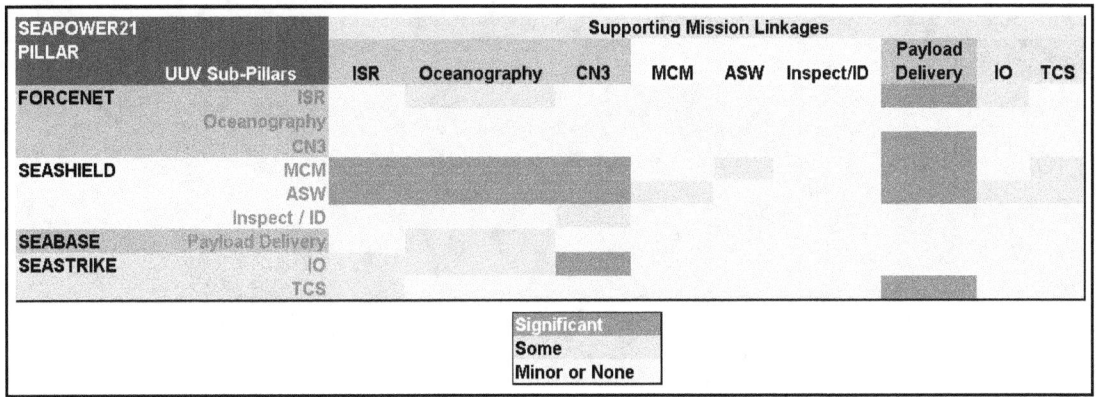

Figure 2-6. UUVMP Sub-Pillar Linkage

As one would expect, each of the defined broad UUV mission areas support a variety of specific missions: ISR, Oceanography, and CN3. Payload Delivery supports multiple missions and Sub-Pillars, specifically: ASW, MCM, SOF, and TCS. ISR, Oceanography, and CN3 are strongly linked to ASW and MCM.

The final set of nine missions, concurred to at the Flag Oversight Board Meeting, henceforth called SEAPOWER21 UUV "Sub-Pillar" capabilities are, in priority order:

1. **Intelligence, Surveillance, and Reconnaissance (ISR)**
2. **Mine Countermeasures (MCM)**
3. **Anti-Submarine Warfare (ASW)**
4. **Inspection / Identification**
5. **Oceanography**
6. **Communications / Navigation Network Node (CN3)**
7. **Payload Delivery**
8. **Information Operations (IO)**
9. **Time Critical Strike (TCS)**

3   UUV Sub-Pillar Capabilities

This Master Plan update builds upon the four Signature Capabilities identified in the year 2000 UUV Master Plan. These capabilities were expected to meet near-term needs and also support evolution to meet future naval requirements. These Signature Capabilities and their expected evolution are shown in Figure 3-1 and described in greater detail in the 2000 Master Plan. They are:

- **Maritime Reconnaissance**
- **Undersea Search and Survey**
- **Communication/Navigation Aid**
- **Submarine Track and Trail**

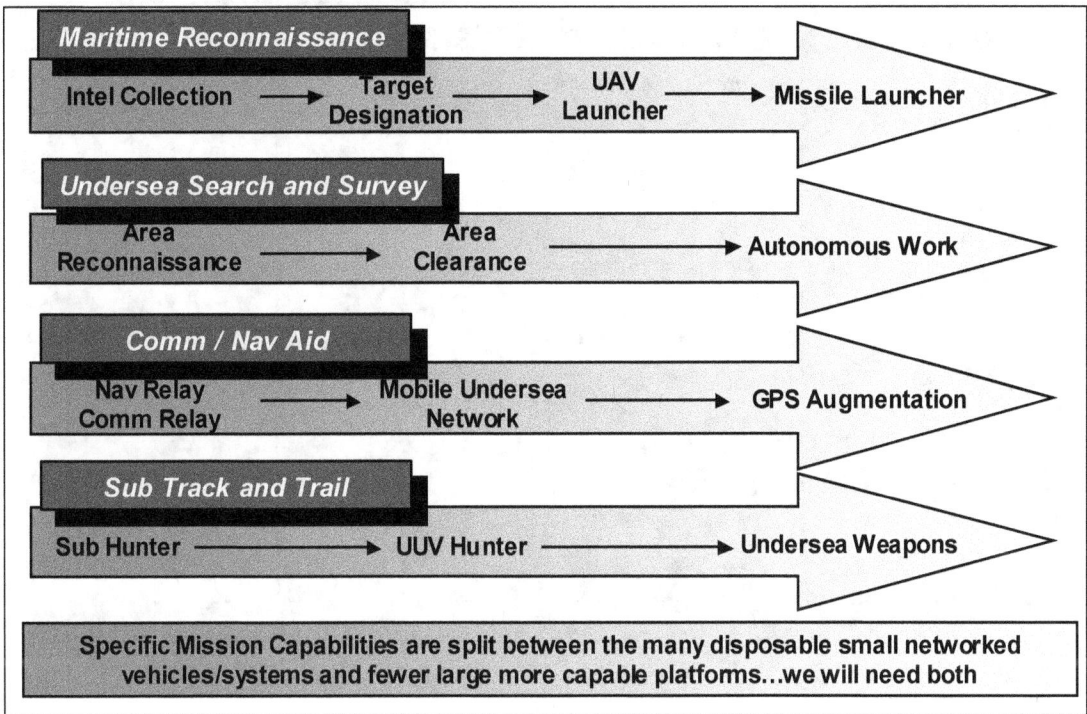

Figure 3-1. Year 2000 UUV Master Plan Signature Capabilities

Maintaining this evolutionary characteristic in UUV development is desirable. The four original UUVMP Signature Capabilities remain relevant and were carried forward in this update, albeit somewhat modified. In general, the mapping of the original Signature Characteristics into the UUV missions or "Sub-Pillar" capabilities introduced in Chapter 2 is as follows:

- **Maritime Reconnaissance → ISR**
- **Undersea Search and Survey → Oceanography and MCM**
- **Comm / Nav Aid → Communication / Navigation Network Node (CN3)**
- **Submarine Track and Trail → ASW**

This mapping is not exact, since some old Signature Capabilities evolved into more than one new mission.

The mapping of the new Sea Power 21 Sub-Pillars to their Sea Power 21 Pillars is shown in Figure 3-2. Each proposed mission evolution and associated technology development to support each Sub-Pillar are discussed in the corresponding section below. Overall technology investment and programmatic roadmaps to achieve these aims are covered in Chapters 4 and 5, respectively.

Figure 3-2. UUV "Sub-Pillars" Mapped to Sea Power 21 Pillars

3.1 Intelligence, Surveillance and Reconnaissance (ISR)

ISR collection has been identified as the number one priority UUV mission, supporting a wide range of other Sub-Pillar Capabilities.

3.1.1 Objective

The purpose of performing ISR missions from a UUV is to collect intelligence data above the ocean surface (electromagnetic, optical, air sampling, weather) and below the ocean surface (acoustic signals, water sampling, ocean bottom equipment monitoring, and object localization) while remaining undetected by the enemy (Figure 3-3). Specific ISR UUV capabilities would include persistent littoral ISR, harbor or port monitoring, Chemical, Biological, Nuclear, Radiological, Explosives (CBNRE) detection and localization, surveillance sensor emplacement, battle damage assessment, active target designation, and launch and coordination of UAVs. These capabilities will substantially improve indications and warning.

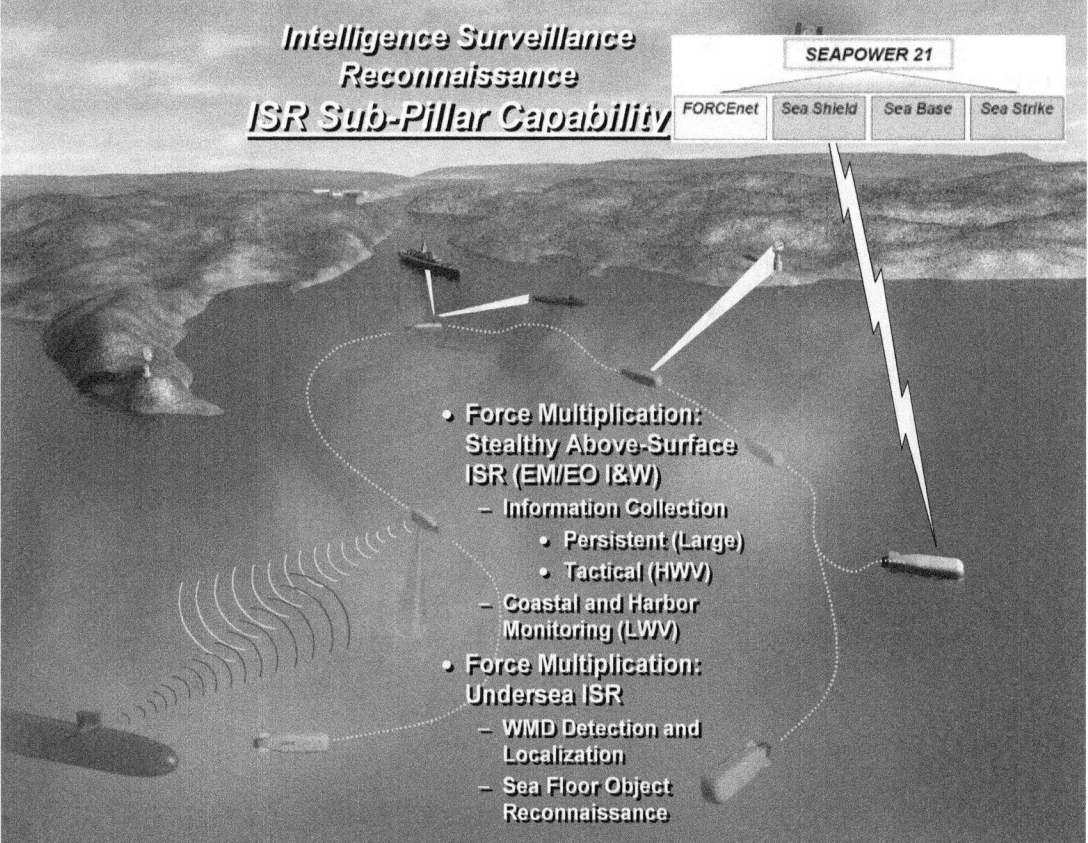

Figure 3-3. ISR UUV Sub-Pillar

3.1.2   Background

UUVs provide many advantages for the ISR mission. ISR UUVs may have a multi-function capability, operate from a variety of platforms, and may enable the collection of many types of data. UUVs could effectively perform these missions in high-risk areas or where hazards to navigation preclude conventional platforms. Long-range UUVs could penetrate such areas, extending the reach of their launch platforms by more than 150 Nmi. UUVs could be launched from a safe standoff distance, transit to the area of interest, and return with, or transmit subsets of, the data collected. This greatly reduces the risk to manned platforms, frees them to perform other high priority missions, and is a force multiplier.

3.1.3   Concept of Operations

The vehicle is launched from its host platform, most likely a submarine, but possibly a surface ship, aircraft, USV or shore facility. The UUV then proceeds to the designated observation area. Once it reaches its OPAREA, it performs the mission, collecting information over a predetermined period of time; autonomously repositions itself as necessary, both to collect additional information and to avoid threats; and provides a persistent presence in the operating area, gathering data for long time periods, perhaps as long as several weeks. The information collected is either transmitted back to a relay station on demand or when "self cued" (i.e., when the vehicle records a threat change and determines that transmission is necessary). In some cases where maximum stealth mission is required at the expense of real-time or semi-real-time transmission, the vehicle will bring the recorded data back to the host platform or to a suitable area for transmission.

3.1.4 System Concepts

A persistent ISR UUV capability can be provided via larger vehicles with significant range, endurance, and capacity for a variety of large payloads. However, credible subsets of this capability can be provided in UUVs as small as 21-inches in diameter, or even smaller vehicles for limited missions. The ISR UUV will have a reconfigurable payload, and thus be able to accommodate a variety of sensors. Table 3-1 summarizes possible operational characteristics for both tactical capability (near-term) and persistent capability (long-term) ISR vehicle concepts.

Table 3-1. ISR Notional Capability

	Tactical Capability	Persistent Capability
Radius of Operation (Nmi)	50-75	75-150+
On station time (hours)	<100	300+
Speed (knots)	3-7	3-7
Nominal Vehicle Size (Displacement in lbs.)	~3,000	~20,000
"In-Air" Mast Mounted Payload (pounds)	<< 100	~100

3.1.5 Technology and Engineering Issues

Critical technology and engineering issues pertaining to the ISR UUV mission capability stem from the need for long transit distances, long times on station, clandestine operations, signature reduction, failsafe vehicle behaviors, vehicle stability, and extended autonomous operation. The requirement for long endurance is difficult but not impossible to achieve when choosing from today's energy source technologies. Long-range communication, though not always required, is an issue. Improvements in current UUV communication capabilities are required. In particular, there is a strong need to increase the bandwidth of communications links while reducing their vulnerability to intercept.

As capability evolves, a major issue to be addressed is the level of autonomy. Ideally, the system will be capable of detecting, recognizing and avoiding threats of a varied and mobile nature. Near-shore obstacles and nets are particularly a challenge (for sensing, autonomy, and net penetration or manipulation). Object avoidance requires a high degree of autonomy, both in threat recognition and the determination of the best means of avoidance. As capabilities improve and the threat evolves, continual enhancements will be required.

Payload development for the ISR capability should largely be concentrated in the effective packaging and integration of sensors. With the large number of sensors desired, it is vitally important that they be packaged with a minimal cross-section (for low detectability). Improvements in individual sensor performance will also be key to overall mission success.

3.2 Mine Countermeasures (MCM)

3.2.1 Objective

MCM supports all three pillars of Sea Power 21 (Sea Strike, Sea Shield and Sea Base). In support of Sea Shield and Sea Base, the objective of this MCM capability is to find or create Fleet Operating Areas that are clear of sea mines without requiring manned platforms to enter suspected mined areas, and to shorten MCM timelines. Further, this capability is required to operate within the near-term Navy force structure and to operate independently of other warfighting capabilities. It is to provide a workable and cost effective solution to a wide range of requirements, as discussed in section 2.3.2. The vision for future mine countermeasures is to field a common set of unmanned, modular MCM systems operated from a variety of platforms or shore sites that can quickly counter the spectrum of threat mines assuring access to our Naval Forces with minimum mine risk.

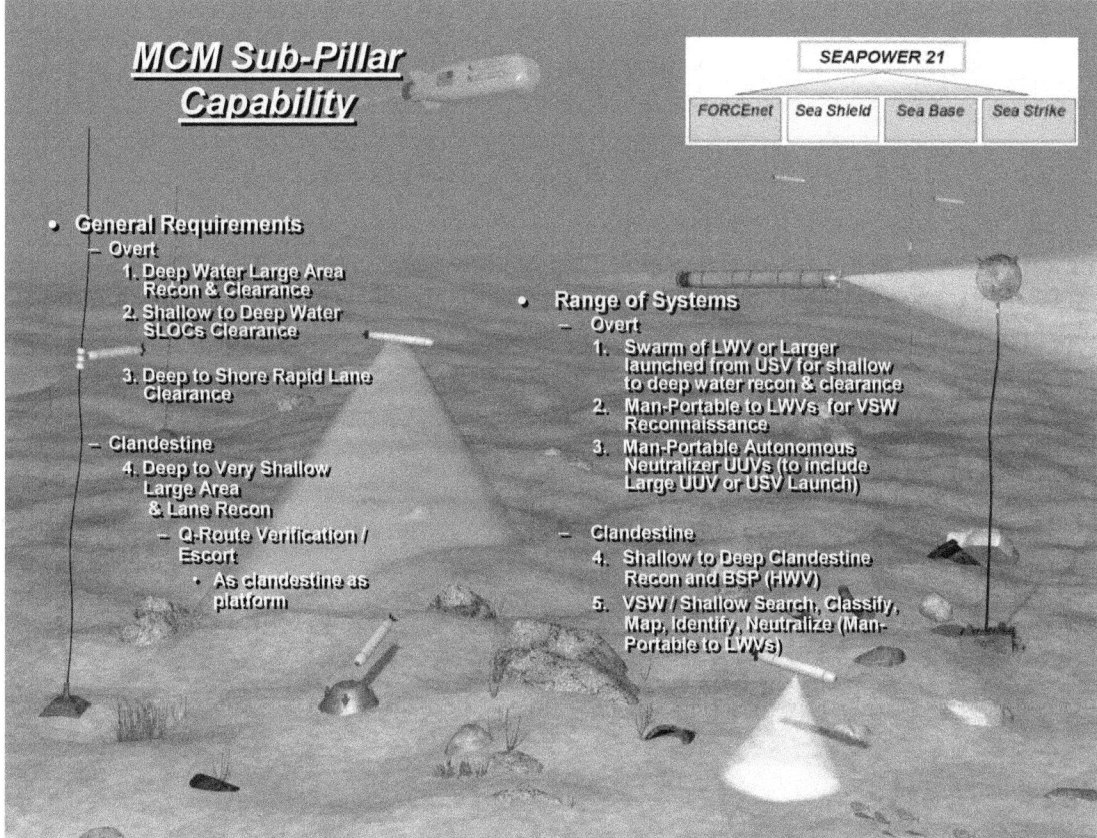

Figure 3-4. MCM Sub-Pillar

3.2.2 Background

MCM is perhaps the most problematic of the missions facing the UUV community and the Navy at large. The proliferation of mine types, their availability to our potential adversaries, their ease of employment over a wide spectrum of water depths, and the "zero-defect" nature of MCM operations combine to make the MCM mission one of the most challenging to the U. S. Navy's access requirements. Figure 3-1 illustrates the counter-mining spectrum used to overcome the complexity of mine threats in the littoral and deep ocean.

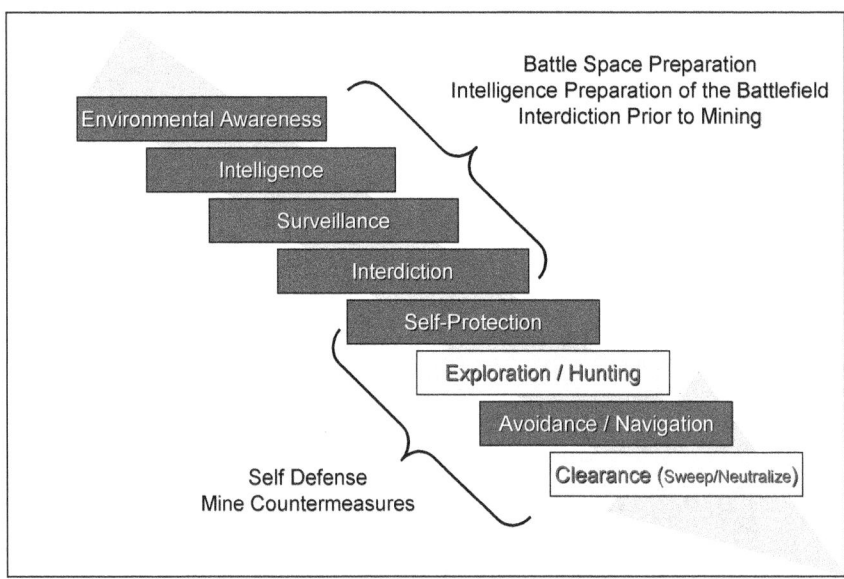

Figure 3-5. Counter Mining Spectrum

On the plus side, small UUVs are being employed successfully in support of MCM missions today (SCULPIN in support of Operation Iraqi Freedom) and larger specialty MCM UUVs are planned for delivery to the Navy in the future. These initiatives are considered to be a good beginning toward a spectrum of UUV-enabled MCM systems that will ultimately enable the Navy to achieve in-stride or near-in-stride access to any of the world's littorals, regardless of the mine threat.

3.2.3 Concept of Operations

In support of this update, a scoping analysis of the overall MCM problem was conducted. This analysis is summarized below.

The functions of MCM that lend themselves to near-term UUV solutions are minehunting and neutralization. These can be further broken down to the following phases:
Detect (D)
Classify (C)
Identify (I)
Neutralize (N)

In order to determine the optimal tactics for employment of UUVs, the multiple phases of the minehunting operation were determined by examining each of the "steps" in varying combinations. The combinations were limited to those that could be accomplished in one or two passes, the steps must be in order of increasing information, and the neutralization step must be performed. Table 3-2 lists the specific Concepts of Employment (COE) assessed.

Table 3-2. Mine Hunting COEs

4 Steps	3 Steps	
DCIN	DCN	
DCI N	DC N	**Key**
DC IN	D CN	**D = Detection**
D CIN	DIN	**C = Classification**
	DI N	**I = Identification**
2 Steps	D IN	**N = Neutralization**
DN	CIN	**Space indicates**
D N	CI N	**a second pass**
CN	C IN	
CN		
IN	**1 Step**	
I N	N	

The multiple steps strategy (detect-classify-identify) for determination of the mine threat was examined to discern an efficient strategy for the employment of UUVs. If multiple sensing steps are desired, they can be performed in a single pass or by multiple passes. Since sensor ranges for each minehunting step vary, multiple steps in one pass require that the vehicle maneuver "off-track" to investigate contacts, lowering the overall area coverage rate (ACR). For multiple pass strategies, one example is that one vehicle would detect and classify with a second vehicle following to identify the objects classified as "mine-like" and to neutralize those deemed to be mines. In the notation shown in Table 3.2 this would appear as DC IN (four steps in two passes).

Intuitively, execution of all phases in a single pass would appear to be the most rapid approach. Therefore, the use of multiple sensing steps in a single pass was examined to determine the impact that off-track maneuvering has on overall performance in terms of ACR. Three key variables were assessed: vehicle speed through the water, the range of the sensors, and the contact density.

It is worth noting that with current and near-term technology, long-range sensors generate less information about their contacts than do the short-range sensors. This results in a higher contact generation rate for a given area. For analysis purposes, the sensor ranges spanned the range from proven to well beyond state-of-the-art and contact generation rates were at the low end for good environments. Higher contact densities will further spread the differences between sensor types, shown in Figure 3-6.

The distribution of sensor contacts was assumed to be uniform over the full range of the sensor. Therefore, for off-track maneuvering COEs, this would require a run perpendicular to the original search path to a distance equal to one half of the sensor range, on average, and back. The resultant ACRs for various sensor speeds, sensor ranges and contact densities are plotted in Figure 3-6.

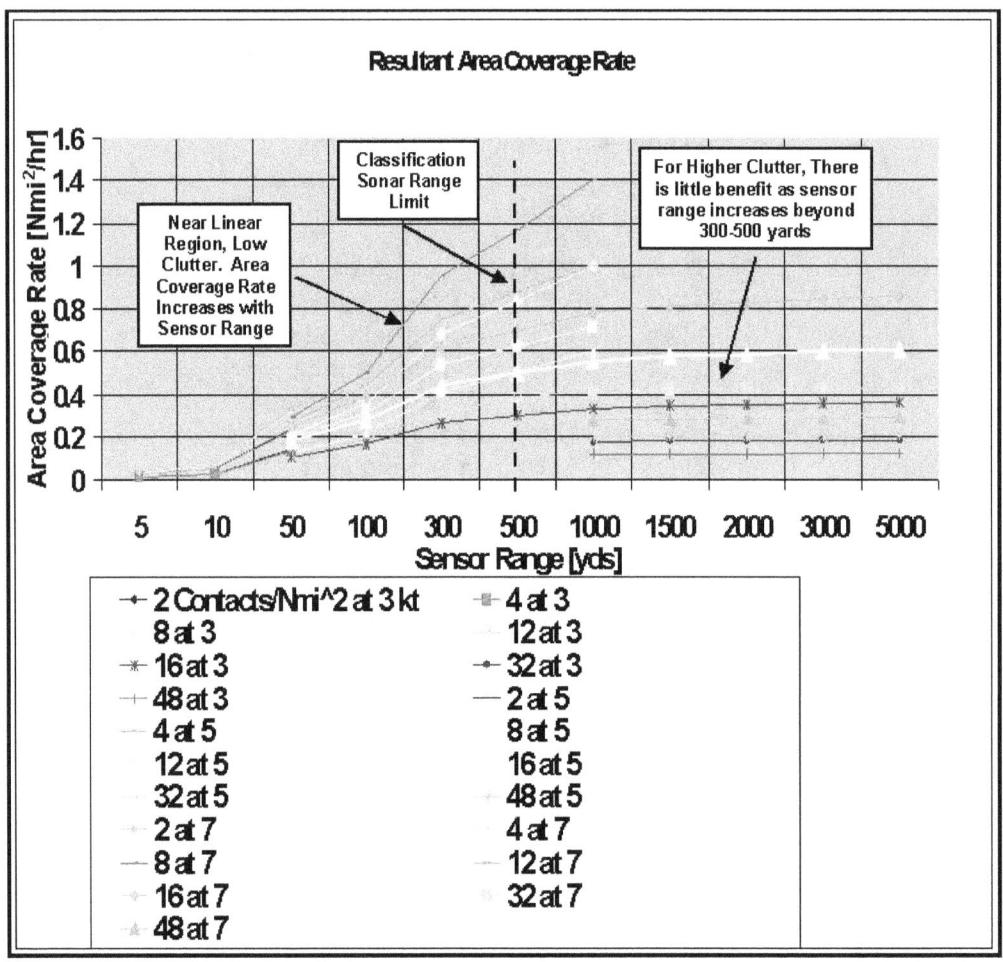

Figure 3-6. Resultant Area Coverage Rate for Maneuvering, Multi-Sensor Systems

The noteworthy feature of this analysis is the flattening of the curves at longer ranges. This indicates that the additional maneuvering caused by the higher contact density of the long-range sensors reaches a point of diminishing returns. For this reason, detection and classification systems that operate both steps in one pass are not recommended for efficient operation against bottom targets, particularly in high clutter environments.

3.2.4 System Concepts

The three COEs that result in systems that can meet the required levels of performance, are designated C IN, CI N, and the CIN. Each of these COEs was examined for applicability to the family of UUVs described in Chapter 5. As a baseline for comparison, the systems were modeled against the worst-case requirement of clearing 900 Nmi^2 in seven days. The sensor parameters used for the analysis are listed below:

- 5 knots speed of advance
- Identification sensor
  - Range = 10 yds
  - False contact density = 2 / Nmi^2
- Classification sensor
  - Range = 500 yds

  o False contact density = 8 / Nmi^2
- Area Coverage Requirement
  o 100% of the area, non-overlapping

In each case it was found that the classification sensor would be too large and require higher platform stability than can be achieved in the Man Portable (MP) class of UUV (UUV classes are defined and discussed in Section 5.1). Therefore the MP class of UUV was not considered as a viable option for this analysis.

Two neutralizers were studied: (1) a stationary bomblet that is placed by a UUV and remotely detonated later using an acoustic command, and (2) an autonomous neutralizer in the class of Man Portable UUVs, essentially a small anti-mine torpedo. The autonomous neutralizer would have to be capable of re-acquiring the target.

The results of this scoping analysis are shown below in Figure 3-7.

C IN
Number of Sorties

Vehicle Class	# of C's	# of C Hours	# of IN's	# of IN Hours	# of N Bomblets
MP	na				
LWV	24	15	161	15	4
HWV	11	33	69	35	8
HWV-Hybrid	3	120	53 **	46	10
Large	4	90	25	97	22
Large - Hybrid	3	120	17	142	32

CI N
Number of Sorties
Using Autonomous Neutralizers transported by UUV

Vehicle Class	# of CI's	# of CI Hours	# of Ns	# of N Hours	# of Auto N
MP	na				
LWV	97	15	284 **	2	2
HWV	42	35	114 **	4	5
HWV-Hybrid	11	132	114 **	4	5
Large	15	97	23 **	18	24
Large - Hybrid	10	145	23 **	18	24

CIN
Number of Sorties

Vehicle Class	# of CIN's	# of Hours	# of N Bomblets
MP	156	10	4
LWV	133 **	12	4
HWV	53 **	30	10
HWV-Hybrid	53 **	30	10
Large	16	98	34
Large - Hybrid	11 **	142	49

** Number of vehicles driven by vehicle payload capacity

CI N

15 Large – 1 Sortie Each
14 HWV – 3 Sorties Each
20 LWV – 5 Sorties Each

CIN

16 Large – 1 Sortie Each
18 HWV – 3 Sorties Each
23 LWV – 5 Sorties Each

- UUV delivery of UUVs to OPAREA required for 2nd and 3rd option for both COEs
- UUV delivery for Autonomous Neutralizers for the CI N COE

Figure 3-7. UUV System Options for MCM Missions

The tables in Figure 3-7 show the number of sorties for each pass in each COEs (number of C's, CI's, CIN's, IN's, and N's). It shows the duration of each sortie in hours (number of C hours, etc.), and the number of neutralization bomblets or autonomous neutralizers.

For the C IN option, the number of C sorties is much less than the other options. However, when considering the number of IN sorties needed to complete the mission, the C IN option becomes sub-optimum. The number of systems necessary for the other two options, CI N and CIN, are comparable. Even fewer UUV assets are required if the UUVs are used for multiple sorties (summarized in Figure 3-7).

As noted in Figure 3-7, the number of neutralization sorties is driven by the UUV's capacity to carry the neutralization devices. For the CI N option, the neutralization step is performed in a separate pass, which has three advantages. The first is that a number of neutralization options become available. The second is that the search vehicles can be much smaller. Finally, there is an opportunity for an operator-in-the-loop to put "eyes" on the image of the identified target prior to neutralization. Neutralization can be performed using autonomous neutralizers capable of reacquiring the targets and can be transported to the OPAREA by UUV, USV, or UAV. USV delivery is attractive because, for example, four 30-knot USVs carrying 135 autonomous neutralizers each, could deliver their entire payload in four hours. This is well within the time requirements for the overt clearance of the large area mission or the clandestine Littoral Penetration Area.

Ultimately the goal would be a fully automated system such as the CIN option, which performs all three steps in a single pass. Reacquisition would not be necessary. The neutralization device would be a bomblet that would have to be effective against bottom as well as volume mines. The bomblet would either be acoustically or timer triggered. The cost of such bomblets would likely be significantly less than the, more sophisticated autonomous neutralizers. Using the HWV and Large UUVs for the placement of the bomblets in shallow water could be problematic.

Additionally, USVs could be used to ferry search UUVs (whether CI or CIN) to and from their OPAREAs (approximately eight 500-pound displacement vehicles per USV, or one to two 3,000-pound displacement vehicles per USV). This would also be an option for the lane or sea-line of communication (SLOC) clearance missions. These missions are typically not well suited to relatively short-range vehicles, due to their long narrow geometries, and long transits for delivery and extraction. The USV ferry method would allow an entire 200 Nmi SLOC to be searched by eight LWVs and neutralized by one USV load of 128 autonomous neutralizers. Therefore, two USVs could accomplish the entire mission, while the host platform stands-off at 90 Nmi.

3.2.5   Technology and Engineering Issues

While the above analysis is not definitive, it clearly indicates that near- to mid-term UUV or UUV / USV technology can realistically contribute to solving the emerging MCM requirements. It also indicates that large UUVs may not be required for these missions. While they certainly could perform the missions, larger numbers of smaller vehicles may be operationally better suited, provide greater mission flexibility, and facilitate graceful system degradation. Clearly, shallower waters continue to be a challenge. The sensor ranges used for the above analysis are not supportable in the very shallow water region (<40 ft.). Other factors: (1) mine types may change, to larger numbers of smaller mines, which would stress the number of neutralizers required, and (2) If neutralization can be limited to defined lanes, the problem becomes more tractable.

The classification sensor performance used for the above analysis is consistent with Synthetic Aperture Sonar (SAS) technology. These systems are degraded in shallow water and as sensor motion increases. While it is desirable to produce one system that will work for all depths, this does not appear feasible in the near- to mid-term. However, the selection of smaller vehicles (500 to 3,000 lbs) for the deep water problem and careful planning could push the technology into shallower waters, as the existing small vehicle technology is pushed out into deeper waters. At some point these systems may merge. For example, the development of a 500-lb. vehicle with a SAS that could be used in a real-aperture mode when in shallow or very shallow water could start to merge these systems. Also, while 500 yards was used as the standard classification range for analysis, this is not a break point. As can be seen in Figure 3-6, any classification range above approximately 300 yards provides good performance. The numbers of sorties or vehicles required to perform these missions will scale approximately with the sensor swath width (this assumes the sensor gap is filled). Sensor size and power consumption become more important features with increased ranges at these levels.

Computer-Aided Classification (CAC) has been demonstrated and in the analysis it is assumed that Computer-Aided Identification (CAI) is an available technology. This technology is necessary to meet the required mission time. The additional minutes necessary for the operator to make an identification on each classified contact can radically change the timeline and number of vehicles required.

Rapid reacquisition and homing on targets with small, low-cost sensors is necessary to produce a cost effective autonomous neutralizer.

Reliable, medium-range acoustic communications and autonomous group behavior will also be necessary to meet the timelines. Repeated surfacing and diving to communicate and problem-solve will waste too much valuable mission time. Gateway systems such as the Communications/Navigation Network Nodes (CN3) described in section 3.5 may be required to facilitate this interaction.

Development of autonomous cooperative behaviors will significantly accelerate MCM operations. Today's autonomous systems consist of individual vehicles that provide data for follow-on decision making (neutralize, avoid) and have limited ability to work with other vehicles. Simple coordinated behaviors have been demonstrated with dissimilar UUVs with one detecting contacts of interest, and passes them to a follow-on vehicle with a sensor for identification or further action. Intelligent behaviors between separate vehicles with different sensors classes will result in a rapid acceleration of the MCM timeline through non-linear methods. Absent this capability, brute force (lots of similar systems uniformly searching and sweeping an area) is the only way to shorten the timeline. Unmanned MCM by 2015 is possible, but this envisioned cooperative autonomy is not likely until further in the future.

Dynamic, in-situ environmental data collected using tactical sensors, like those used on UUVs, is referred to as Through-the-Sensor (TTS) Environmental Data Collection (EDC). Accurate near real-time TTS EDC is a critical part of the MIW's IPB Phased Concept, as illustrated in Figure 3-8.

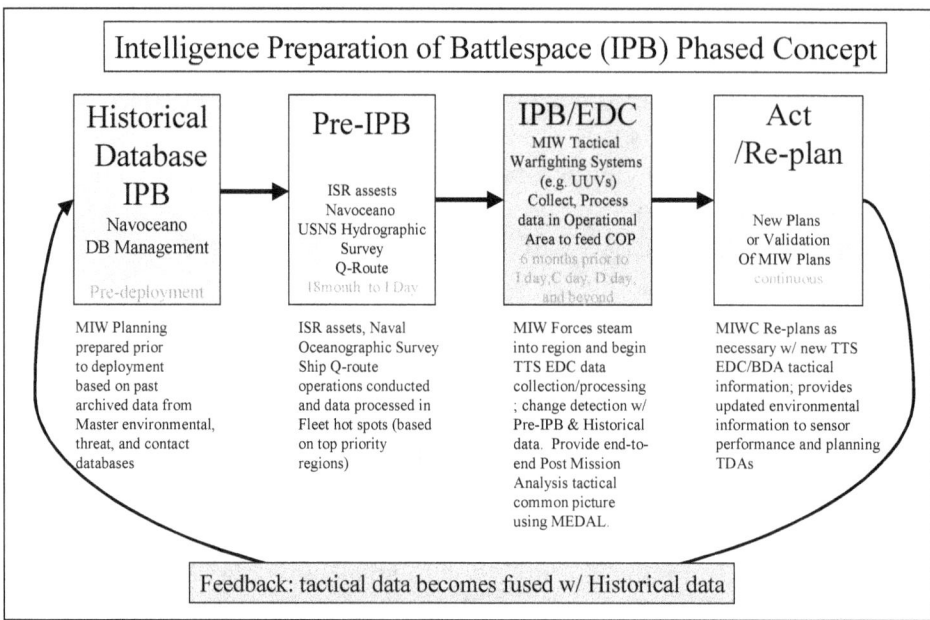

Figure 3-8. MIW Through-the-Sensor (TTS) Environmental Data Collection (EDC)

IPB is needed to determine the right tactics, mission planning, asset and sensor management, sensor and system performance, and battle damage assessment. IPB minimizes the time required to perform the MCM mission and successfully provides a common undersea picture (CUP) to Fleet assets and Joint commanders through the Mine Warfare and Environmental Decision Aids Library (MEDAL). MEDAL integrates IPB, mission planning and evaluations, situational awareness, and command and control tools to support the MIW Commander, organic and dedicated MCM operators, Strike mining planners, LCS Mission OIC and all naval forces requiring mine warfare situational awareness.

3.3 Anti-Submarine Warfare (ASW)

The Sea Power 21 Sea Shield ASW Sub-Pillar is illustrated in Figure 3-9. UUVs will complement and extend existing anti-submarine warfare capabilities.

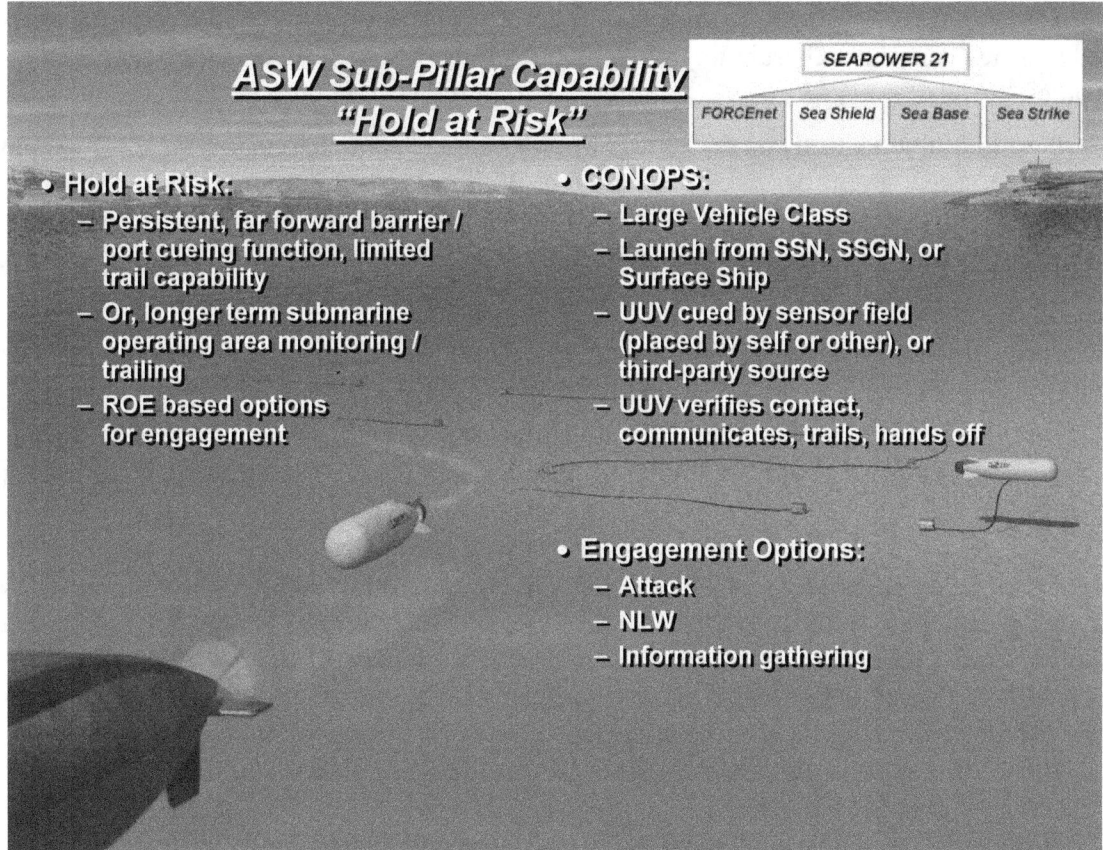

Figure 3-9. ASW Sub-Pillar Concept of Operation "Hold at Risk"

3.3.1 Objective

As noted in Section 2.3.3, this capability focuses on the Task Force ASW "Hold at Risk" scenario, in which a UUV, aided by third-party cueing, monitors and tracks the submarine traffic through an adversary port egress or other choke point. The objective of this capability is to patrol, detect, track, and hand off adversary submarines to U.S. Forces using UUVs. A further objective is to perform this function under any ROE without taking actions that inadvertently advance the stage of conflict. Given the potential restriction of access due to bathymetry or threat, the fact that undersea forces may be the only forces available early enough, and the desire to track submarines regardless of the stage of conflict, the UUV is a leading candidate for the "Hold at Risk" task.

3.3.2 Background

It is vitally important that the U.S. Navy be able to achieve and maintain access to all the world's littorals at the times and places of its choosing. In view of the increasing submarine threat from our potential adversaries, it is critical to establish and maintain a highly effective ASW capability. Current ASW techniques are effective, but there are several factors that point to UUVs taking on a complementary ASW role in the future:

Due to the lack of necessity for an ocean transit or large magazine (payload), adversary submarines can be much smaller than U.S. submarines, and thus operate more easily in shallower waters. Due to the bathymetry and local knowledge, it is likely that these submarines can and will submerge near their homeports and outside the reach of U.S. Forces.

Furthermore, due to ROE or the proliferation of other technologies, air superiority may not be assured at all stages of conflict. Without local air superiority, inherently clandestine undersea vehicles (manned and unmanned) may be the only undenied forces early in the conflict capable of accomplishing the IPB required in a timely manner and with reasonable risk.

In ASW, especially in submarine vs. submarine engagements, it is best to be the first submarine to attack. Dominance is not possible in reactive anti-submarine warfare.

The number of submarines that may be 'surge' deployed near-simultaneously by our adversaries mandates a force multiplier to enhance the efforts of existing ASW assets.

3.3.3 Concept of Operations

The development of a completely independent, fully autonomous, long-term UUV tracking capability with large area search is not considered to be feasible or practical in the mid-term. Even short of this ideal capability, however, there are several ASW capabilities that UUVs can provide as significant complements to existing ASW forces. For example, focusing on specific areas through which the enemy must pass (as opposed to large area search) is a necessary simplification. This simplification in CONOPs allows relatively simple UUVs (compared to manned ASW assets) to hold an enemy "at risk." UUV applications that complement ASW are addressed below, from technically easiest to most difficult to implement, given these simplifying assumptions.

The basics of the ASW "Hold at Risk" capability are shown in Figure 3-9. The UUV and its users are assumed to have access to some type of background intelligence on the home port and nominal readiness of adversary submarines, but are unlikely to have knowledge of specific sailing dates and times. The precise course of departure from the port to the 12 Nmi limit and the location of the dive point are also variables. Due to the possibility of adversary (local) air superiority and the limitations of the bathymetry around ports of interest, candidate UUV launch platforms may have a closest point of approach that is still a substantial distance away from the adversary's dive point.

The UUV is launched and transits into the intercept area—typically a port egress route or choke point—where it establishes contact with a source of off-board cueing (e.g., other UUVs, a pre-existing deployed sensor field, or other third party source) and monitors that source for cueing. Typically the UUV will maintain its position relative to the cueing sensor in a low-energy "loiter" mode, which will facilitate its ability to remain on station for extended periods. When cued, the UUV takes up position and maneuvers to verify the cue's initial classification. If successful, the UUV reports to its decision authorities. UUV options at this point, from easiest to hardest technically, include:

- Return to cueing barrier in "loiter" mode to wait for the next cue,
- Employ lethal weaponry against the adversary, and
- Employ non-lethal weaponry (NLW) against the adversary.

Establish intermediate-term track of the target while avoiding counter-detection and communicating to its controllers that a track has been initiated, with periodic updates. At the end of the tracking phase (due to handoff, energy exhaustion, or orders from its controllers), the UUV would break contact and transit to a rendezvous location based on the initial sortie plan or as updated during communication intervals.

Later, perhaps after a significant loiter period, the UUV would be recovered or replenished to enable another mission.

Alternate ASW Sub-Pillar options include:

- Having the UUV employ its own autonomous or semi-autonomous sensor field (e.g., Advanced Deployable Systems (ADS), Deployable Autonomous Distributed System (DADS), or Remote Deployable System (RDS)).

- Having the UUV establish a barrier patrol without the benefit of cueing sensors. This option is only appropriate in very restricted choke points, since the UUV's energy availability will not allow it to execute a significant search rate for an extended time period and still maintain adequate reserves for the tracking part of the mission. Options that can mitigate this situation somewhat include use of vehicle-mounted non-traditional tracking (NTT) sensors to enhance effective search rate, and use of NLW to aid its own tracking efforts (and those of others).

ROE and CONOPs development are required to enable some of the options noted above. Specifically:

- Permitting the employment of NLW early in the pursuit, eliminating the requirement for longer-term track, and enabling immediate handoff to other ASW assets.

- Permitting the use of lethal weaponry from the UUV, either semi-autonomously (man-in-loop) or autonomously (UUV makes the decision). In addition to CONOPs and ROE attention, this option would require technical and operational assurances to protect friendly forces operating in the vicinity.

Any of the above options–except for the stand-alone search and track option–individually or in combination, can reduce the endurance requirements on the UUV substantially by mitigating the requirement to maintain track of the target submarine for a significant time. These changes would also reduce the complexity associated with UUV autonomy for the tracking mission, but greatly increase the autonomy complexity associated with release of weaponry, lethal or otherwise.

3.3.4　System Concepts

"Submarine Track and Trail" was the least defined of the four Signature Capabilities in the 2000 UUV Master Plan. Since that time, great strides have been made–analytically, technically, and in Navy focus–toward making the ASW mission a reality in the future. The specific system concept is pending resolution of technical issues, decisions on launch platforms (submarine, surface ship, or both), and resolution of engineering issues associated with those platforms. Work in the Analyses of Alternatives (AoAs) and other studies in support of littoral combat ship (LCS), SSGN, and UUV programs is beginning to address those platform engineering issues, while several Office of Naval Research

(ONR) Future Naval Capability (FNC) studies and bilateral technical agreements are progressing. The expected system parameters are listed in Table 3-3.

Table 3-3. Notional Capabilities, Hold At Risk ASW

Radius of operation (Nmi)	10-100+
Endurance (hours)	100-400
Patrol Area –Choke Point (Nmi)	5-50
Speed Range (knots)	3-12
Displacement (pounds)	~20,000

A large UUV housing several sensor suites with an advanced energy and propulsion capability is envisioned to provide this ASW capability. The sensor suite would likely include: a passive acoustics sonar, either conformal or towed; a NTT sensor (used for the initial detection or as an aid in maintaining track); and a short-range very high frequency, low-probability of intercept (LPI) sonar for obstacle avoidance and close tracking. The UUV would have extensive communications capabilities. These would include acoustic communications and satellite communications (SATCOM) and may include others, such as one-way "bread crumb" radio buoys or retractable tethered radio buoys. The advent of the mission reconfigurable approach to Navy UUV implementation also raises the possibility of the UUV laying its own cueing field prior to conducting the mission described above.

3.3.5 Technology and Engineering Issues

Technology issues associated with this capability include: communications, energy, propulsion, sensors, and autonomy. In the area of propulsion and energy, the speed and endurance requirements for the tracking portion of ASW will be significant challenges. Non-acoustic sensors show promise for ASW and require additional development for UUV applications. Engineering issues exist with the launch and recovery of large UUVs.

Another issue worthy of reiterating in this section is vehicle communication. Potential options for vehicle periodic reporting include use of a "floating wire" type Satellite Communications (SATCOM) system, as this would enable transmission of quarry parameters without breaking contact. Additional communications options include: (a) disposable one-way communications buoys that would be programmed and deployed at appropriate times, and (b) retractable floating buoy antennae that can be deployed and retracted at will. It is expected that technical and operational advances in submarine communications at speed and depth will feed similar advances for UUVs, with appropriate scaling.

Although the ASW Sub-Pillar capability presents various technology challenges—most of which are being worked at ONR and in other technical programs–this capability is very high payoff and subsets of this capability would provide immediate force multiplication. The ASW Sub-Pillar capability also leads to growth into other future mission areas, such as semi-autonomous or completely autonomous engagement, which will ensure continued dominance.

3.4 Inspection / Identification

3.4.1 Objective

The Inspection / Identification Capability will support Homeland Defense (HLD) and Anti-Terrorism / Force Protection (AT/FP) needs. It will be able to perform a rapid search function with object investigation and localization in confined areas such as ship hulls, in and around pier pilings, and the bottoms of berthing areas. As stated in Commander Explosive Ordnance Disposal Group TWO's letter dated June 13, 2003, *Explosive Ordnance Disposal (EOD) Anti-Terrorism / Force Protection (AT/FP) Unmanned Underwater Vehicle (UUV) Mission Requirement Priorities,* the goal is to be able to "rapidly reconnoiter areas of concern (e.g., hulls, port areas, and other underwater areas) and to detect, investigate and localize unexploded ordnance (UXO) objects that impose a threat to military forces, high value assets, navigable waterways, and homeland security."

Current performance objectives (*Coast Guard Requirements 2004*) for this mission include the following:

> Hull Search: 1000-foot ship, 100-foot beam, 50-foot depth in 8 hours
> Pier / Harbor Area Search: 1500-foot pier, 50 feet wide, and 100 feet deep in 24 hours

These area coverage rates are approximately three times those currently available with divers and other systems, such as ROVs. UUVs provide a means to address these objectives in a cost-effective fashion, reserving divers and ROVs for the more complex tasks requiring real-time human intervention.

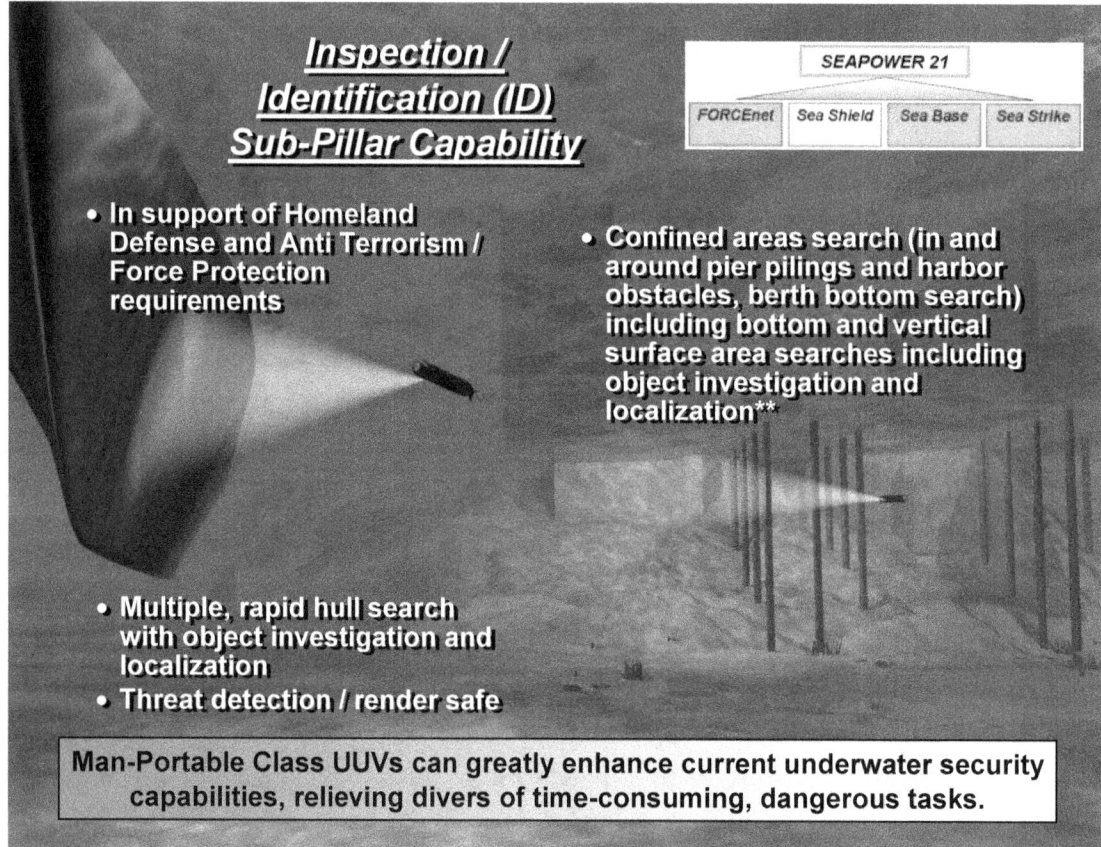

Figure 3-10. Inspection / Identification Sub-Pillar Background

While the detailed inspection / identification mission has been addressed on several occasions over the past 15 years, it is only with the recent emergence of the Global War on Terror (GWOT) and Homeland Defense that it has gained a military priority. The Underwater Security Vehicle (Fletcher, 1990) program demonstrated the use of an ROV for swimmer detection, identification and interception in a pier-side environment. There have been both military and civilian programs demonstrating the operation of ROVs on ship hulls for ship husbandry and non-destructive test purposes. These efforts all feed into the current requirements for the inspection / identification capability.

In 2002, the Navy's *Small UUV Strategic Plan* (28 June 2002) delineated three basic mission tasks for UUVs to address: Very Shallow Water Mine Countermeasures (VSW MCM), Surface Mine Countermeasures, and EOD. The Commander, Explosive Ordnance Disposal Group Two issued a letter in June 2003 which provided direction to minimize EOD diver exposure to ordnance hazards through the search-detect-identify-neutralize missions. To this end, three specific UUV missions were identified: (1) rapid hull search and target localization, (2) harbor area search and target localization, and (3) open water search and target localization. The EOD UUV Analysis of Alternatives study team operated from April 2003-March 2004, examining the roles that a UUV might play to supplement their expanding mission needs. The Inspection / Identification task can also be expanded to include the inspection of other water-based assets.

3.4.2 Concept of Operations

The full Inspection / Identification mission is currently outside the realm of UUV operational capabilities. However, a UUV can provide a useful asset to current hull and pier inspection operations, by performing the broader area surveys, freeing divers to concentrate on the more complex areas and designated targets that require real-time human judgment. It is critical that the UUV system be compatible with other systems in use, so that the data may be quickly interpreted and acted upon. A possible operational scenario might be as follows:

1) Deliver UUV system to the operational area
2) Input known data on environment (charts, hull model, etc) into system for UUV mission planning
3) Develop inspection plan
4) Deploy support equipment (navigation transponders, communication relays, etc.)
5) Deploy vehicle to run programmed path and collect sensor data
6) Monitor real-time or near real-time communication from vehicle containing sensor data content
7) If a target of interest is detected, relay coordinates and any additional information to the dive team or ROV operations team
8) Continue mission
9) Recover vehicle
10) Redeploy as necessary

The Inspection / Identification vehicle must be able to operate in a range of pierside environments. Table 3-4 outlines some basic capability requirements needed for this mission.

Table 3-4. Inspection/Identification Capability Criteria

Criteria	
Depth	10-100 feet
Current	3 knots
Standoff	0 + Nmi
Area Covered	1500 feet x 200 feet
Max Weight	100 + pounds
Time on Station	12 hours
Deployment Platform	7-meter RHIB or Shore Deployed

3.4.3 System Concepts

The Inspection / Identification system is intended to be a man-portable system, easily deployed without need of special handling equipment. The system must be highly maneuverable, able to operate in a cluttered, complex environment. Unlike many UUVs which are built for hydrodynamic efficiency, the Inspection / Identification system must be able to hover and orient itself to obtain identification quality images of the areas being inspected. Some of the critical subsystems include:

Sensors: Identification quality images must be obtained of relatively small targets (2"x4"x9"). While video is highly desirable, it is often of limited use in the low-visibility harbor environment. High-frequency acoustic systems such as the high-frequency side scan and acoustic lens forward-looking sonars may provide good imaging tools in the harbor setting.

Navigation: A high degree of accuracy (±0.5m) is required for the location of potential targets found in the inspection process. The ship hull / pier side environment is difficult for traditional navigation methods (acoustic, magnetic), yielding the need to address the problem with an integrated approach of inertial, acoustic, and other methods.

Communication: Real-time or near real-time communication of sensor data from the vehicle is required to effectively perform the inspection / identification mission.

Human Interface: Due to the rapid deployment requirements for this system, it is imperative that the human interface be clear and intuitive. As the UUV system will be a single component in the overall mission package, it is particularly important that the data interfaces be compatible with the other tools in use.

3.4.4 Technology and Engineering Issues

The technology and engineering issues associated with the Inspection / Identification capability are largely driven by the complexity of the ship hull / pier side environment and the need for rapid response to identified targets. Typically the harbor environment is extremely cluttered with poor visibility and acoustic characteristics. This poses challenges to the execution of the technical requirements, particularly in the areas of navigation and communication.

Navigation: The ship hull / pier side environment is difficult for traditional navigation methods (acoustic, magnetic), yielding the need to address the problem with an integrated approach of inertial, acoustic, and other methods to get the high degree of accuracy required.

Communication: Real-time or near real-time communication of sensor data from the vehicle is required to effectively perform the inspection / identification mission. Component technologies such as acoustic communications, radio-frequency (RF) relays, and expendable fiber optic cables exist that may address these needs, but they have not yet been integrated into an operational system for this application.

Maneuverability: The vehicle must be sufficiently maneuverable to maintain a proper sensor orientation relative to the hull or structure of interest. This requires a higher degree of control than is often found in more conventional cylindrical UUVs.

Autonomy: Ideally, the vehicle will be able to operate effectively in the complex, cluttered environment without the need for direct human supervision. While this remains in the future, the ability of the vehicle to independently identify targets of interest would greatly reduce the operator workload.

Sensors: Lightweight, affordable sensors that can discriminate between objects of interest and objects inherent to ship hulls and piers will enable UUVs to communicate data to operators, allowing for continued survey or initiation of action to render safe potential threats, including unexploded ordnance and weapons of mass destruction.

Compatibility with other Systems: Due to the complexity of the operating environment, it is doubtful that a UUV will be able to perform the entire inspection / identification mission independently. It is therefore critical that the system and the data it collects be complementary with the other systems in use such as divers, marine mammals, and remotely operated vehicles. The navigation and communication systems in particular must be compatible with other systems in use. Development and adaptation of the FORCEnet standards will ensure the compatibility with current and emerging systems.

3.5 Oceanography

Oceanography includes collection of hydrographic, oceanographic, and meteorological data in all ocean environments. Oceanography supports real-time operations as well as IPB for expected operations. Oceanographic data and environmental products are provided in near real-time for tactical support, archived for long-term support, and provided in rapid-turnaround mode for operational battlespace preparation.

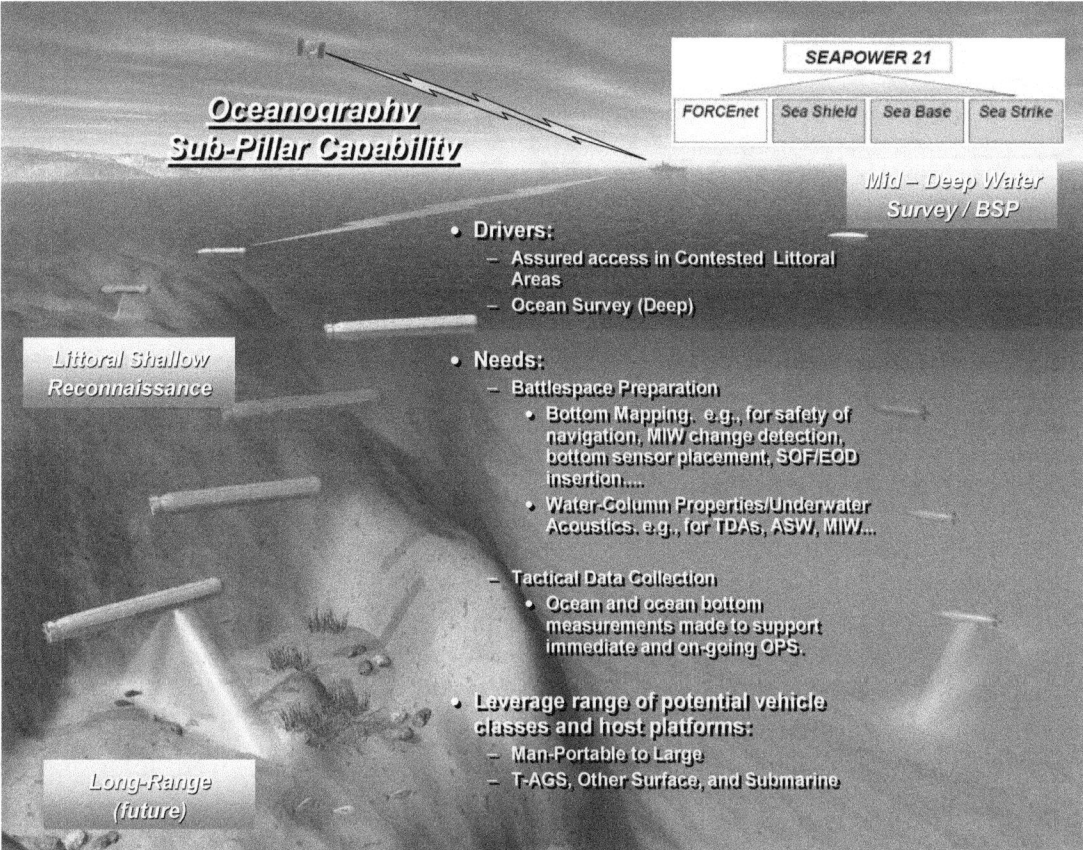

Figure 3-11. Oceanography Sub-Pillar

The oceanographic function is described herein as a dedicated set of UUV capabilities. However all UUVs collect oceanographic data in order to function. Adherence of UUV developers to established standards for data formats would allow efficient use of these data to augment that collected by dedicated oceanographic platforms.

3.5.1 Objective

Oceanography ranges from broad reconnaissance of large littoral undersea areas to detailed characterization of specific battlespace areas collecting high quality, accurately positioned data. There is a need to perform these missions in areas where battlespace dominance has not been achieved. The focus is on the littoral, but a deep-water survey capability is required for bottom characterization to accomplish cable route pre-installation and inspection. The shallow-water littoral region survey is useful in aiding navigation or projecting sensor performance. This type of mission may be best accomplished using small UUVs or gliders.

UUV technology is a force multiplier to manned platforms and is essential to meet critical oceanography requirements. The predominant driver for adopting UUV technology for ocean survey is to increase the timeliness and cost effectiveness with which the fleet can acquire affordable, near real time data at required temporal and spatial sampling densities. Used in conjunction with remote sensors, other ocean data, and models, UUV-acquired data provides warfighters with critically required foreknowledge of environmental parameters such as bathymetry, tides, waves, currents, winds, acoustic propagation characteristics, locations of hazards to navigation, and other objects of interest.

3.5.2 Background

Over the last four years, prototype UUVs have been fielded for the purpose of oceanographic reconnaissance. The UUVs were designed to collect high-quality, precision-located environmental data in the littoral regions of the world. Additionally, a capability was instituted for full-ocean-depth (20,000 feet) rated dives with integrated physical oceanography and bottom-mapping sensors. UUV capabilities also supported two types of missions: independent physical oceanographic data collections and side-scan sonar bottom-mapping surveys. Smaller vehicles are now available to execute shallow-water hydrographic and coastal oceanographic surveys.

3.5.3 Concept of Operations

All naval platforms; manned and unmanned, surface, air and undersea; gather Oceanographic data to varying degrees in parallel with their other missions. Examples include: submarine Precision Underwater MApping (PUMA), MIW assets, and ASW operations. Dedicated oceanographic operations occur worldwide; these operations will be augmented by UUVs operating from oceanographic survey (T-AGS) ships and ships of opportunity. Medium sized UUVs will support reconnaissance in shallow to mid-depth (continental shelf) regions. Smaller UUVs will be employed for use from hydrographic survey launches, other small craft, and aircraft. These UUVs will operate in localized areas. Other small, dedicated UUVs will drift with the currents or glide using batteries or energy extracted from the oceans while profiling to gather ocean survey data over very large areas. These vehicles will extend applications of Profiling

Autonomous Lagrangian Circulation Explorer (PALACE) and other drifting buoys. Later when large vehicles have been fielded, oceanography payloads may be incorporated into these UUVs to provide a long-range capability.

The oceanography mission must directly (and often simultaneously) support multiple warfare areas. For example, ocean survey vehicles will gather bottom object information supporting Mine Warfare (MIW) and acoustic information supporting ASW. Under FORCEnet, common data elements and archives will allow for rapid access to all information for the areas of interest.

3.5.4 System Concepts

No single system will meet all of the oceanography requirements affordably. Structure and operations requirements for littoral missions differ significantly from those for deep-water missions. Commonalities of sensors, interfaces, and data formats mitigate the resource impacts of diverse requirements. Both shallow and mid-to-deep water capabilities are needed as described below and in Table 3-5.

Table 3-5. Oceanography Notional Capabilities

	Shallow Water	Mid-Deep Water Survey
Depth (ft.)	0-100	50 - Deep
On station time (hours)	10-12	30 - 50
Nominal Displacement (lbs.)	<100	~3000
Deployment Platform	Small Boat	T-AGS 60, Littoral Combat Ship

Shallow Water Small UUV: This system will be used in both denied and contested areas to extend reach. As a force multiplier, it will provide 2 - 3 times greater collection area for same number of personnel. It will provide full bottom coverage to meet the International Hydrographic Organization's standards for navigation quality charts.

Mid to Deep Water Survey / Battle Space Preparation UUV: This provides primary denied area, clandestine survey and oceanographic data collection capability, with cross-platform launch and recovery capability. Data collected will support stringent navigation quality chart production and oceanographic data collection requirements, and also will be used to support ASW, SOF, Expeditionary Warfare (EXW), Ship to Objective Maneuver (STOM), and MIW change detection. The sensor suite will include full multibeam, side scan (e.g., SAS), forward looking / obstacle avoidance sonar capabilities, sub-bottom profiler, and oceanographic data collection suite.

3.5.5 Technology and Engineering Issues

Deep-water ocean surveys can be executed using existing technology. However, to meet existing ocean survey requirements will require years of dedicated ocean survey operations worldwide using T-AGS 60, and requirements are increasing.

Contested area surveys can also be executed using existing technologies. However, UUVs reduce the level of risk and provocation. In addition, UUVs offer advantages in terms of area coverage rate and cost per Nmi^2.

Deep water UUVs will provide a substantial increase in collection capability for each UUV over present deep-towed systems. However, to achieve the full benefits of UUVs in both deep and shallow water, advances in technology are necessary. Particular technology constraints on oceanography UUV operation include needs for long-range transit and surveys, high-resolution data in both shallow and deep water, precise positioning, and rapid data recovery and transfer.

Tactical use will require reliable high-bandwidth communications over 10-100 miles. Some long-range UUV missions will require significant navigational accuracy without surfacing the vehicle. Several technologies have the potential to meet these requirements, including moored or mobile acoustic transponder networks, and onboard comparison of terrain with archives of bottom features from acoustic imagery. The Communication / Navigation Network Node (CN3) capability discussed in Section 3.6 addresses many of these requirements.

Operational requirements mandate increases both in mission range and endurance. Higher-density energy storage and means for extracting energy from the ocean environment are essential. Miniaturized, low-energy sensors are a priority. Undersea docking stations for recharging batteries and extracting data should be viewed as long-term options. Glider UUV technology, especially with air-deployment capability, will be used to provide sustained and continuous oceanographic monitoring, significantly enhancing current drifting buoy programs.

3.6 Communication / Navigation, and Network Node (CN3)

The Communication / Navigation Network Node (CN3) will be the enabling undersea node of the Net-centric Warfare Sensor Grid. As such, it will serve as the implementation of FORCEnet for UUV applications and forms the interface to the Global Information Grid (GIG). It will provide networked connectivity across multiple platforms and the ability to provide navigation aids on demand. Navigation and communication components developed for this capability will become integral parts of, or support other UUV systems fielded in the future.

3.6.1 Objective

The objective of the CN3 is to provide a low-profile communication and navigation relay function for a wide variety of platforms. As a communications relay, the primary focus is on providing the connectivity to FORCEnet for underwater systems. Links would be established with underwater stations, other platforms, and SATCOM capabilities as shown in Figure 3-12. The advantages offered by using a UUV include extended standoff distances and greater accessibility. CN3 will provide submerged communications to undersea platforms in areas not otherwise available. Potential users include other UUVs, submarines operating at speed and depth, Special Forces units, and any other application where low-visibility communication is desirable.

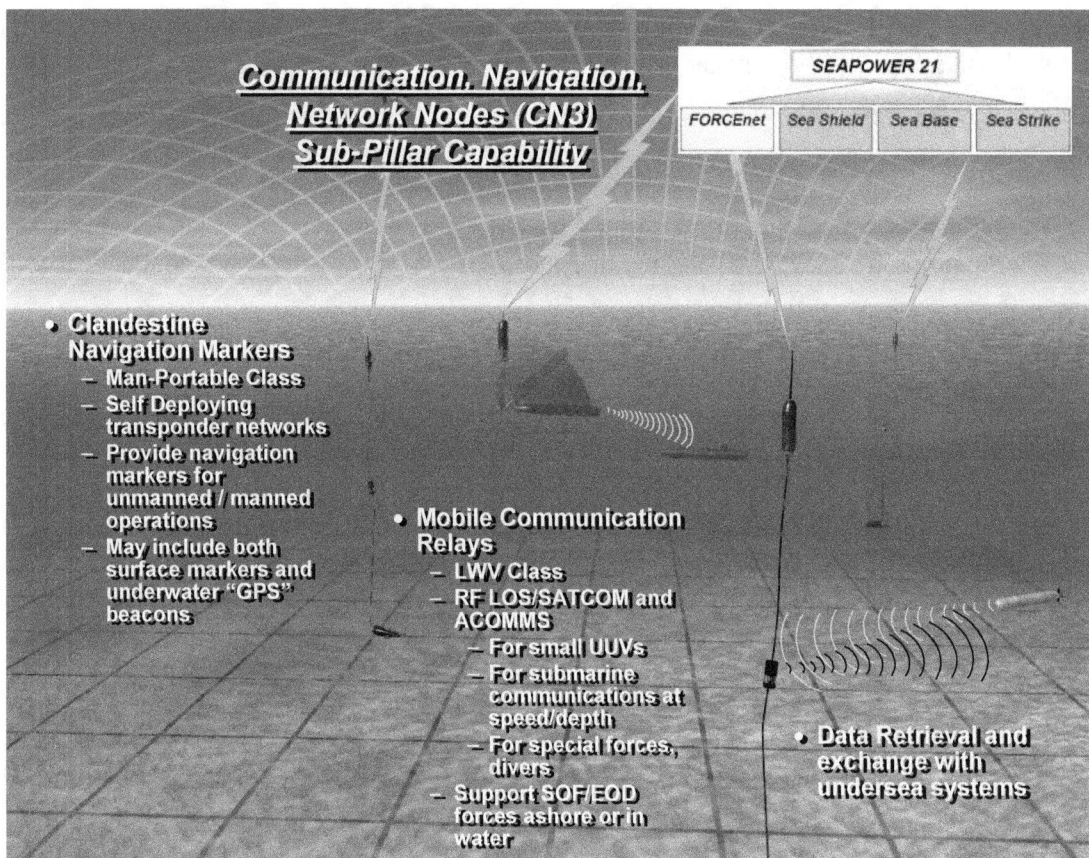

Figure 3-12. Communication/Navigation Network Nodes (CN3) Sub-Pillar

As a navigation aid, the CN3 UUV is envisioned as an on-site on-demand reference point for subsea or surface operations. Pre-positioned, either just prior to, or well in advance of planned operations, the vehicles will provide reference beacons (visual, radar, or acoustic) for other UUVs, submarines, SOF, or surface operations. These could take the form of lane designators, undersea mileposts, or supplementing or replacing conventional navigation means. In critical situations, the CN3 UUV could provide an above- or below-water navigation capability equivalent to GPS accuracy without the need for continuous direct satellite communications. CN3 UUVs will also aid less-capable UUV systems, providing a mobile geographic reference system. An immediate application would be a self-deploying navigation transponder for use by SOF vehicle systems.

3.6.2 Background

The CN3 capability is a support function enabling other systems to perform their missions more effectively (see Figure 3-12). These range from providing efficient over-the-horizon navigation beacons for SOF operations to connection with the undersea FORCEnet.

One immediate application of the CN3 would be a self-deploying transponder network to support near-shore SOF and EOD missions; such tasks are now performed with small manned vehicles. Currently, forces in rubber boats deploy the transponder field–putting men in high threat areas. A CN3 UUV could be launched from a safe distance, transit to the operations area using GPS, and then deploy itself as a transponder node for operations. The mission assets could then transit into the area, orient themselves to the network, and perform their mission without the need to expose human operators.

Looking to the future, the growing emphasis on networked systems will require multiple undersea components. UUV systems will be FORCEnet compatible, able to connect with sensor fields, arrays, other UUVs and multiple platforms. The flexibility provided by UUV systems is especially important for mobile, dynamic systems such as submarine communications at speed and depth, operation of UUV swarms, and connection with SOF.

3.6.3 Concept of Operations

The general CN3 CONOPS is to provide on-the-spot connectivity and navigation capability for a variety of platforms. This is envisioned as both a stand-alone capability and also as a component of other Sea Power 21 UUV capabilities. The modules developed for the CN3 UUV will also support the navigation and communication requirements of ASW, MCM, and SOF missions. Table 3-6 below summarizes some CN3 UUV notional capabilities covering both the expendable self-deploying transponder and the mobile communication relay.

Table 3-6. Communication/Navigation Network Node (CN3) Notional Capabilities

	Expendable Navigation Marker	Mobile Communication Relay
Radius of Operation (Nmi)	10 - 20	250
On station time (hours)	72	72
Endurance (operational) (hours)	5	72
Speed (knots)	2 - 5	2 - 5
Nominal Displacement (pounds)	< 100	500

On-demand navigation references could be useful to platforms of all types. The vehicles would be programmed to transit to desired marker locations. Delivery of the vehicles could be performed by a variety of platforms (including aircraft), well in advance of the intended need. The vehicles would then proceed to the designated locations, navigating inertially or with GPS. They would sit quiescent until the time of operation (either preset or on-command). Once activated, the vehicles would deploy navigation beacons, either pop-up buoys, acoustic transponders, or other markers. Once their operations are complete, the vehicles would have the options of scuttling or returning to a home base for recharging and reuse.

For use as a communications relay, the UUV would be outfitted with the desired mode(s) of communication: optical fiber spool and connector, acoustic modem, laser communication, RF, or SATCOM antenna. The vehicle is launched from its host and makes the desired connection, either with a subsea fixture, another platform, or the surface for SATCOM transmissions. The data exchange would take place–either one-way or two-way–with minimal impact on host platform operations. Once communications are concluded, the vehicle could either be scuttled or recovered. While this function is most obviously an asset to submarines, SOF, other UUVs, or surface ships requiring connectivity to a subsea entity could also use it effectively.

3.6.4 System Concepts

Many basic system features are common to both the communication and navigation functions of the CN3 UUV. The basic vehicle configuration is seen as a small, low-cost system, potentially expendable under certain operational conditions. Ideally the UUV will be adaptable to a variety of platforms, requiring minimum support equipment for launch. Beyond the vehicle itself, many of the subsystems (communication and navigation modules) developed for this capability will become integral parts of the other systems discussed.

The communications portion is seen as a versatile link, able to provide connectivity through a selection of modes. It would likely contain an acoustic modem, relaying communications between vehicles or from a subsea network. A vehicle could carry an antenna suitable for communications direct to other platforms or via satellite, providing a safe standoff capability from the host platform and allowing a full range of contact through conventional communication channels. Laser and fiber optic communications have also been demonstrated on UUVs—these too could be incorporated as another means of communication. Ideally, a stand-alone communications relay could be easily configurable with a variety of communications modes, readily adaptable to operational needs.

The navigation system component is relatively straightforward, requiring mainly the ability and endurance to navigate to a desired location. This would most likely entail the use of GPS navigation, whereby a relatively small UUV can maintain a low enough profile on the surface to avoid detection. The vehicle payload would be the navigation beacon, either an underwater acoustic transponder or a pop-up buoy. The buoy might include both visual and radar targets, enabling its use under a wide variety of conditions. Sizing of this system would be largely dependent on the buoy requirements and the desirability of being able to transit significant distances. A small expendable version would be an asset to SOF forces, relieving the need to manually deploy transponder fields in hazardous areas.

For both the communication and navigation functions, whole networks of systems can be envisioned, with CN3 UUVs providing connectivity to FORCEnet. Depending on the mission requirements, a variety of platforms may be employed as the CN3 UUV, including small UUVs, gliders, solar powered UUVs, and gateway buoys (Figure 3-13).

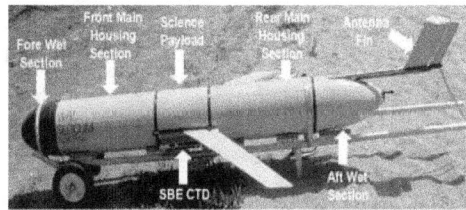 

Figure 3-13. Potential Non-Conventional CN3 Platforms: Glider or Solar Powered

3.6.5   Technology and Engineering Issues

Of all the Sea Power 21 UUV Capabilities discussed, the CN3 is the most technologically ready for development.   There are no critical path developments preventing the construction and deployment of the initial systems described. All of the key technologies have been demonstrated as feasible by individual autonomous systems. Enhancements to the integral functions, however, will permit the systems to achieve a wider range of operational capabilities.   System complexity and long-term deployment will be key factors in the development of cost effective systems.

Much work is currently ongoing on undersea communication modes. Particularly in the area of acoustic communications, advancements are desirable in bandwidth, data rates, range, security, and reliability. Networking is critical, and the compatibility conferred by the adoption of open architectures and communications standards is a must.

The key engineering issue for the employment of these systems is largely one of the infrastructures required.   These vehicles are seen as the means of connecting to the undersea FORCEnet grid, but this must first exist before they can be of use. There must be stations available that are readily compatible with the vehicles and reliable over long periods of time. Issues such as long-term immersion and biofouling must be considered for extended use. Both the vehicles and all supporting infrastructure must be designed to operate in a rugged and reliable manner for long duration deployments.

3.7   Payload Delivery

3.7.1   Objective

The objective of the Payload Delivery Capability is to provide a clandestine method of delivering various payloads to support other mission areas. The missions supported would include MCM, CN3, ASW, Oceanography, SOF Support, and TSC (Figure 3-14). The CONOPS for each of these mission areas are discussed in each of their representative sections.

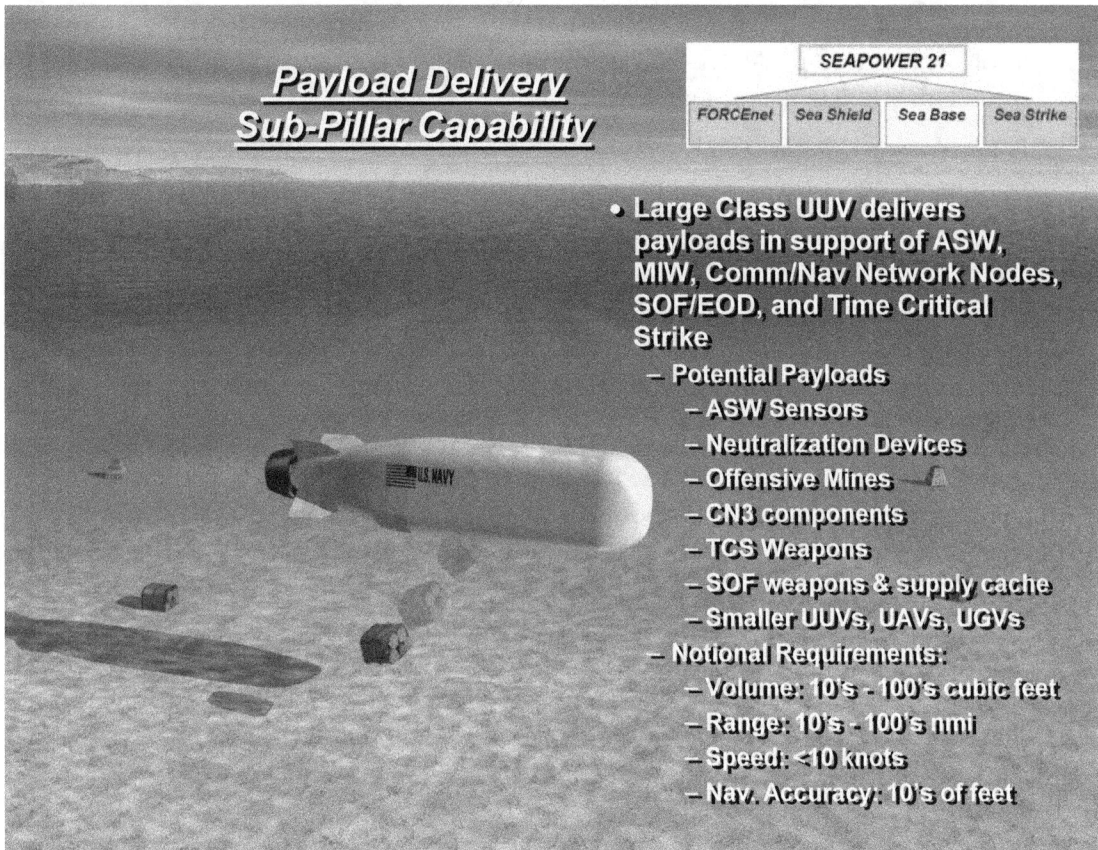

Figure 3-14. Payload Delivery Sub-Pillar

3.7.2 Background

Payload delivery is not a mission in itself, but is necessary to support a number of other mission areas. As a payload delivery platform, the UUV would essentially act as an underwater truck. The UUV would provide the energy, navigation, autonomy, and payload deployment systems necessary to support the other missions.

3.7.3 Concept of Operations

The concept of operation for payload delivery depends on the particular mission being supported. Since a payload delivery UUV would be large and would include fairly robust autonomy, navigation, energy, and propulsion, in most cases vehicle recovery would be desired following delivery of payloads. Some of the mission areas and concepts of operation include the following:

MCM: To support the MCM mission, a large UUV would provide the capability of inserting smaller devices into forward areas. It could deploy sensors that would detect mine laying operations, a swarm of smaller vehicles that perform mine reconnaissance, or mine neutralization devices or mine neutralizing UUVs.

Oceanography: To support Oceanography, a large UUV could deploy sensors used to collect long-term oceanographic data. It could also deploy a group of smaller vehicles to survey shallow water.

<u>ASW</u>: To support the ASW mission area, a large UUV could deploy underwater sensor arrays used to detect the passage of enemy submarines. A UUV could also deploy either lethal or non-lethal weapons.

<u>CN3</u>: To support the CN3 mission area, a large UUV could deliver underwater communications nodes or acoustic-to-RF communications transponders. A UUV could also deliver transponders used to provide accurate navigation for other manned and unmanned platforms.

<u>SOF Support</u>: A large UUV could be used to resupply SOF personnel with weapons, food, batteries, fuel, and other supplies. It could also carry transport devices (i.e. motorcycles or all-terrain vehicles (ATVs)) increasing the mobility and operating range of the forces.

<u>Time Critical Strike (TCS)</u>: To support the TCS mission, a UUV could deliver an underwater weapons cache or buoyant missile launch capsules that would loiter in place awaiting launch instructions, or the UUV itself could carry the weapons and loiter.

3.7.4 System Concepts

The Payload Delivery capability requires a large vehicle with significant range, endurance, and payload capacity. Table 3-7 summarizes possible operational characteristics for a Payload Delivery vehicle.

Table 3-7. Payload Delivery Notional Capability

Radius of Operation (Nmi)	>100
On station time (hours)	Minimal for delivery, 90 days for loiter
Payload (cu ft)	~30 (+ External stores)
Speed (knots)	2-5
Nominal Displacement (pounds)	~20,000

3.7.5 Technology and Engineering Issues

Critical technologies needed to support UUV Payload Delivery missions include: energy density for clandestine long-range transit, vehicle reliability, accurate navigation, vehicle ballasting and control systems, and underwater payload delivery systems.

3.8 Information Operations (IO)

Information Operations (IO) plays a key role in the Sea Strike pillar of Sea Power 21.

3.8.1 Objective

The objective of Information Operations is to "deceive, deter and disrupt our enemies." These operations can use virtually any platform, weapon or means. UUV capability to operate clandestinely in shallow waters and areas too hazardous for a manned platform makes them ideally suited for several IO missions which could not be performed by other platforms. The two IO roles that UUVs seem best suited for are use as communications or computer node jammer and employment as a submarine decoy.

3.8.2 Background

The technology to support IO exists or can be easily leveraged from other sub-pillars. The Navy has long employed submarine simulators as ASW targets. These are considered UUVs. The basic targets had little if any intelligent autonomy, navigating a pre-assigned route while transmitting the acoustic and magnetic signature of a selected submarine.

3.8.3 Concept of Operations

An IO UUV could also be used as a platform to jam enemy communication nodes. The natural stealth and small size of a UUV allow it to operate in littoral areas that would be difficult or impossible for other platforms to reach. This enables the transport of a transmitter and antenna to close proximity of susceptible communications nodes. Injection of false data would be much more difficult, requiring either a reliable communications link with the vehicle or a sophisticated degree of autonomy which would recognize and act on the opportunity to inject the erroneous data. Enhancements in the autonomy and sophistication of UUVs may make this a feasible mission in addition to jamming.

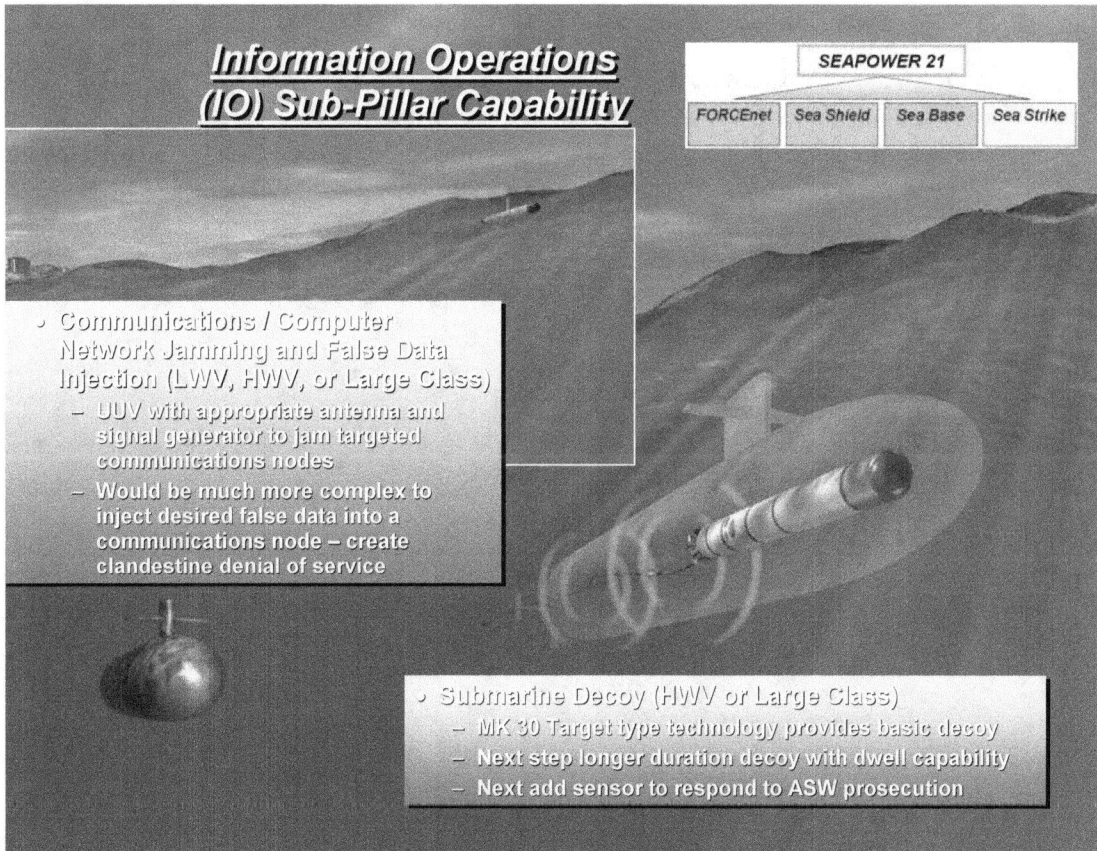

Figure 3-15. Information Operations Sub-Pillar

Submarine decoys could be used in several different scenarios. A simple decoy could be used to transit an area known to have enemy ASW forces or sensors. It could transit a pre-programmed path designed to attract attention and enemy response. A more sophisticated vehicle could be designed to react to prosecution, becoming evasive and perhaps gradually lowering its acoustic signature and causing the prosecuting forces to lose contact. It could then go dormant for a period of time and then repeat its decoy action. These submarine decoys could be used to pulse enemy ASW forces causing them to expend effort that would otherwise be used to endanger friendly submarines. In addition, these decoys could be used to cause the enemy to alter its plans, perhaps deciding not to sail its ships from an area thought to be in danger from the spoof submarine.

3.8.4   Technology and Engineering Issues

There are no critical path developments preventing the construction and deployment of systems similar to those described for the IO missions. Submarine targets and decoys could be used in their current forms for the submarine decoy mission. Enhanced range and autonomy would increase their operational utility. The same is largely true of the jamming mission. Although UUVs have not been built for this mission before, all the necessary component technology is mature enough for a rudimentary jammer to be built and deployed.

3.9   Time Critical Strike

Time Critical Strike (TCS) is in the Kinetic Effects portion of the Sea Strike pillar of Sea Power 21. TCS provides the capability to deliver ordnance to a target with sensor-to-shooter closure measured in seconds, rather than minutes or hours. These operations can use virtually any platform, vehicle, or weapon within the battlespace. Launching a weapon from a UUV, or a UUV delivered weapon cache, allows a launch point closer to the target resulting in quicker response time for prosecution. It also moves the "flaming datum" away from high value platforms so that their positions are not exposed.

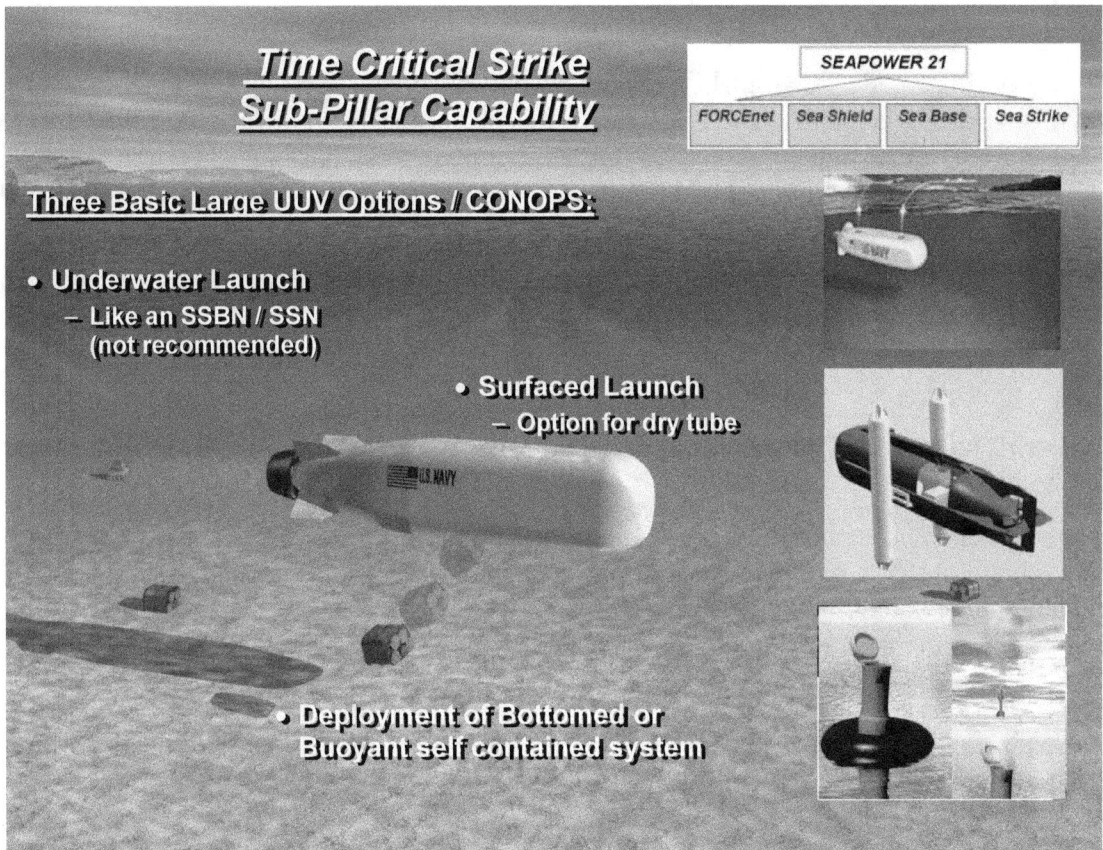

Figure 3-16. Time Critical Strike (TCS) Sub-Pillar

3.9.1 Objective

The objective of TCS is to deliver kinetic effects weapons against multiple targets of interest within extremely short periods of time. The capability to operate clandestinely in shallow waters and areas too hazardous for a manned platform and to loiter clandestinely for extended periods of time, makes UUVs ideally suited for certain aspects of the TCS mission. The two TCS roles that UUVs seem best suited for are as a delivery platform for leave-behind weapon caches and as a remote weapon launch platform for close-in attack against time-sensitive targets.

3.9.2 Background

TCS is one of the lower priority missions for UUVs. An autonomous weapon launch capability is controversial, and man-in-the-loop control of weapon launch will be required for the foreseeable future. However, UUVs can provide low-risk, high payoff augmentation to strike missions, providing an ability to clandestinely deliver weapons to close-in launch points.

The TCS mission was ranked as moderately suitable for UUVs. When viewed as a specialized "Payload Delivery" mission where the payload is a missile, the TCS mission was kept on the list of recommended UUV sub-pillar capabilities.

51

3.9.3 Concept of Operations

UUVs could provide TCS capability using several different CONOPS. The first scenario involves missile launch from the UUV. In this scenario, the vehicle is launched from a platform of opportunity, either a surface ship or submarine, and transits to a predetermined launch point. The UUV anchors or loiters in the area awaiting the launch command. When commanded, the UUV either:

- Launches the missiles while submerged, similar to an SSBN or SSN,
- Surfaces to launch the missiles,
- Or releases a buoyant missile capsule that floats to the surface and launches the missile

When all missiles are launched, the UUV transits to a recovery point for refurbishment and reloading.

The submerged launch option is not highly recommended because of the complexity of the vehicle systems required, i.e. floodable launch tubes, trim and ballast systems, and reliable underwater communication systems as well as a sea-adapted missile. All options in this scenario place the burden of the operation on the UUV.

The second scenario is similar to the first, except that the UUV surfaces to launch missiles. This avoids the complexities of submerged launch and communications. The UUV would anchor or loiter in the launch area with an antenna on or above the surface awaiting a launch order. When alerted, the UUV could raise a higher bandwidth antenna to receive any new targeting information. When ordered the vehicle would surface and launch its missiles under the control of a remote operator.

The third scenario involves a UUV that carries the missiles as a deployable payload. The UUV is launched from a platform of opportunity outside of the battlespace. The vehicle transits to a predetermined location where the weapon cache is deployed. The weapon cache rests on the bottom or floats on the surface until commanded to launch missiles. The UUV returns to the host for another weapon cache module. This scenario places the burden of the operation on the deployed weapon cache. The UUV is simply the delivery truck.

3.9.4 System Concept

The TCS capability can only be accomplished using a large vehicle with significant range and a large payload capacity. Table 3-8 summarizes possible operational characteristics for a TCS vehicle concept.

Table 3-8. Time Critical Strike (TCS) Sub-Pillar

Radius of Operation (Nmi)	>100
On station time (hours)	>>100
Payload (cu ft)	~30 (+ External stores)
Speed (knots)	2-5
Nominal Displacement (pounds)	~20,000

3.9.5   Technology and Engineering Issues

Critical technologies needed to support UUV TCS missions include: secure and clandestine underwater communications, depending on the specific concept of operation; energy density for long range transit and loiter; weapon cache, missile, and weaponized buoy launch techniques; and vehicle reliability.

4 UUV Technology and Engineering Issues

Effective use of UUVs requires appropriate technology development, sound engineering, and systems integration. Efforts must be made in all of these areas in order to achieve the Sea Power 21 Sub-Pillar capabilities and goals of this Master Plan.

4.1 Technology Area Risk Assessment

The Sub-Pillar UUV capabilities will be realized by capable and mature technologies and engineering infrastructure. Not all the envisioned UUV missions can be performed today; some mission capabilities will require new technologies and engineering solutions. The process diagramed Figure 4-1 was used to facilitate the assessment of technology importance, needs, and maturity. The goal was to develop recommendations for future research, development, test and evaluation efforts.

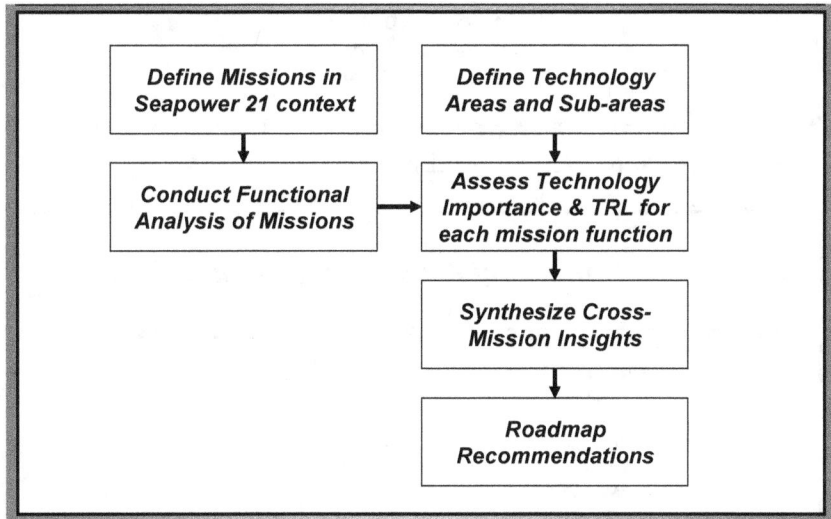

Figure 4-1. Technology Assessment Process for Master Plan Update

After the UUV missions were defined, a functional analysis was performed. The Sub-Pillar capabilities were decomposed into component functions such as vehicle control, sensing, communication, engagement / intervention, and support. Technology areas (and sub-areas) needed to enable these functions were then defined, e.g., sensors, communication, navigation, energy, data processing, etc. as shown in Figure 4-2 and Figure 4-3.

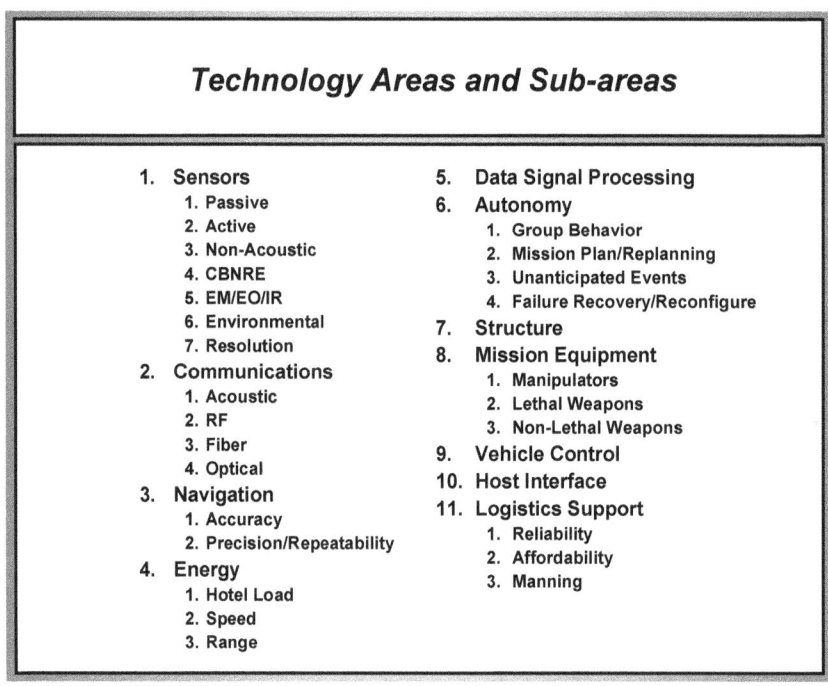

Functional Analysis of Sub-Pillars

1. **Control**
   1. **Maneuver**
      1. Transit
      2. Search
      3. Loiter
      4. Close Target
      5. Homing & Docking
      6. Reacquire
   2. **Human Systems Interface**
   3. **Signature**
      1. Acoustic
      2. Magnetic
      3. Electric
      4. Pressure

2. **Sense**
   1. **Active Search**
      1. Detect Classify
      2. Avoid Obstacles
   2. **Undersea Imaging**
      1. Identify
   3. **Locate**
   4. **Above Surface**
      1. Pressure
   3. **Communicate**
      1. Intermittent
      2. Continuous
      3. Networked
   4. **Engage / Intervention**
      1. Payload Delivery
      2. Payload Retrieval
      3. Jam/Passivate

4. **Engage / Intervention** (cont'd)
   4. **Interact**
      1. Precision Work
      2. Sample
   5. **Attack**
      1. Non Lethal Weapon
      2. Weapon

5. **Support**
   1. **Launch & Recovery**
      1. Overt
      2. Clandestine
   2. **Turnaround**
      1. Rearm
      2. Repair

Figure 4-2. Sub-Pillar Functional Analysis

Technology Areas and Sub-areas

1. **Sensors**
   1. Passive
   2. Active
   3. Non-Acoustic
   4. CBNRE
   5. EM/EO/IR
   6. Environmental
   7. Resolution
2. **Communications**
   1. Acoustic
   2. RF
   3. Fiber
   4. Optical
3. **Navigation**
   1. Accuracy
   2. Precision/Repeatability
4. **Energy**
   1. Hotel Load
   2. Speed
   3. Range

5. **Data Signal Processing**
6. **Autonomy**
   1. Group Behavior
   2. Mission Plan/Replanning
   3. Unanticipated Events
   4. Failure Recovery/Reconfigure
7. **Structure**
8. **Mission Equipment**
   1. Manipulators
   2. Lethal Weapons
   3. Non-Lethal Weapons
9. **Vehicle Control**
10. **Host Interface**
11. **Logistics Support**
    1. Reliability
    2. Affordability
    3. Manning

Figure 4-3. Sub-Pillar Areas

For each sub-pillar capability, a matrix was filled out which provided a method for evaluating both the importance of the function and the Technology Readiness Level (TRL) for the particular capability. The TRLs, as defined by the Department of Defense (DoD), are shown on the left side of Figure 4-4. An example matrix, for the CN3 mission area, is shown on the right side of Figure 4-4. The matrices developed for the nine Sub-

Pillars were analyzed individually then combined to provide an overview of the technology readiness for UUV usage as shown in Figure 4-5.

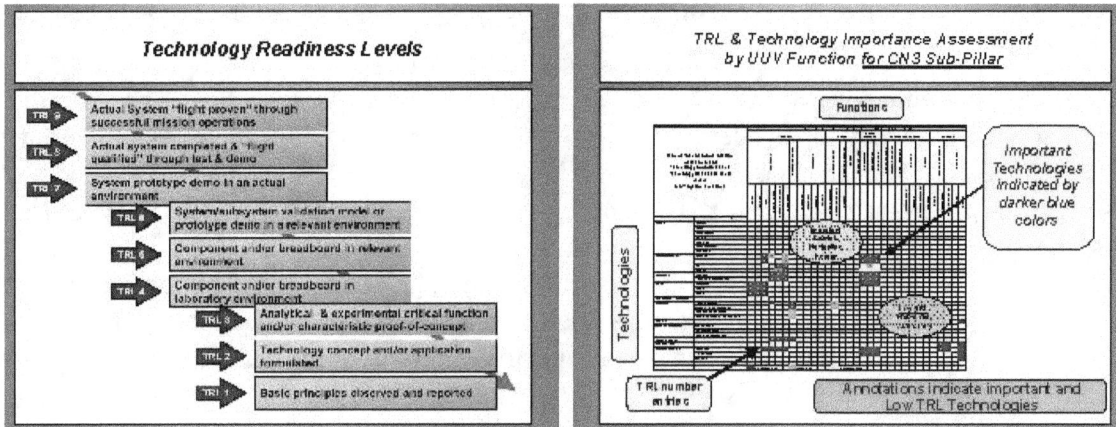

Figure 4-4. TRL & Technology Importance Assessment Example

Based on this analysis, technologies assessed as both important and low TRL for more than one Sub-Pillar and therefore, requiring additional research, development, test and evaluation (RDT&E) investment are Autonomy, Sensors, Energy, Communications and Networking, and Engagement / Intervention. Technologies assessed as adequate to pursue development of Sub-Pillar Capabilities are Data Signal Processing, Logistics Support, Navigation, and Vehicle Control.

	Maneuver	Human Systems Interface	Signature	Sense	Communicate	Engage/Intervention	Support/ Launch & Recovery
Sensors	6.4	9.0	5.9	6.7		6.5	7.4
Communications	7.0	7.8	6.0	7.3	6.2	5.3	6.5
Navigation	6.8	8.0		7.0	7.4	6.0	7.5
Energy	4.8		6.7	7.6	8.4	5.0	7.4
Data Signal Processing	5.8	8.0	6.0	5.8	7.5	4.0	8.0
Autonomy	4.9	4.4	3.0	5.0	4.0	4.0	4.7
Structure	7.5		6.3	8.0		4.8	7.7
Mission Equipment		6.1	7.0	6.5	3.3	4.9	7.1
Vehicle Control	7.1	5.0	9.0	5.5		4.6	7.8
Host Interface	8.8	8.0	9.0	9.0	9.0		7.5
Logistics Support	7.2	7.0		7.3	6.7	4.3	7.0
		Average TRL =	1	to	5		
		Average TRL =	5	to	7		
		Average TRL =	7	to	9		

Figure 4-5. Technology Readiness Levels of Sub-Pillar Functions vs. UUV Subsystems

4.1.1 Autonomy

Autonomy issues are key to all the UUV missions. The need for long-term independent operation is the basis for the ISR, ASW, and MCM missions. These require the ability to transit long distances, detect, assess, and avoid potential threats; and collect information independent of direct human operation. Another aspect of autonomy issues is the operation and coordination of multiple vehicles. This is key to accomplishing large scale MCM and oceanography tasks, both for object sensing and intervention and ocean survey applications.

The area of autonomy and control is a major research area for all UUVs, whether military, commercial, or academic in origin. Areas requiring development cover the spectrum of UUV operations. Data from UUV sensors must be collected, evaluated and sorted for importance both as a mission product and as it impacts on vehicle operation for the remainder of the sortie. It must autonomously recognize data representing a threat or calling for a change in its initial sortie plan and then respond appropriately. Unanticipated events or data may require that the vehicle report its findings immediately, abort a mission, or shift its initial sortie priorities. The sophistication of autonomy needed for successful UUVs is significantly greater than for in other unmanned systems due to the difficulty (or, in some cases, impossibility) in maintaining a communication link between human controllers an the vehicle. These areas all require continuing work to develop the robust capacity required by the Sea Power 21 Pillars.

4.1.2 Energy

Energy has long been a major consideration due to its effect on the ultimate performance of extended vehicle missions. For air-independent power, the energy source becomes a major factor in the design and efficiency of vehicle systems. For all operations there is a desire to minimize the size, cost, and signature of the energy and propulsion system. Missions such as ASW and ISR with high speed and endurance requirements will require more sophisticated energy systems, such as fuel cells and hybrid systems.

4.1.3 Sensors and Sensor Processing

All of the missions described depend on the effective use of sensors, most particularly the MCM, ISR and ASW capabilities. Development in the sensor arena needs to be concentrated in increasing area coverage rate (ACR), improved classification and identification capabilities, non-traditional tracking techniques, and multi-threat chemical, biological, nuclear, radiological, and explosive (CBNRE) sensors.

Synthetic Aperture Sonar (SAS) is the current leading candidate to best meet the requirements of the MCM mission. SAS promises to provide both increased area coverage rate (or a reduced required number of UUVs) and increased resolution. A vehicle with SAS would likely have a three to five-fold improvement in classification area coverage rate and a three-fold improvement in resolution.

The performance of current passive ASW sensors at apertures possible from medium-sized UUVs is suitable for the ASW "Hold at Risk" mission. However, the real breakthrough ASW sensor for UUV applications may be non-acoustic. This technology is not as strongly aperture dependent as acoustic sensors and can therefore be exploited in smaller systems. Regardless of the sensor choice, sensor algorithm processing must be automated so that the sensor can be used in a "track, but do not be counter-detected" role. Some passive homing technology can be transferred from torpedoes, but implementation of the "track, but avoid" tactic will be challenging.

Sensor processing and the automated decision making associated with the processing remains a developmental area for both MCM and ASW. For MCM the principal risk will be the autonomous processing of sonar and optical images to classify mine like objects and identify mines. For ASW, the biggest challenges are associated with autonomous processing, target recognition, countermeasure rejection, target motion analysis (TMA), and tactics.

All of the missions require a degree of precision navigation, from the long-distance transits of ISR missions to the precise target localization of the Inspection / Identification missions. Achieving this is not a risk area unless the use of GPS is precluded. When restrictions exist, navigational problems can be addressed via use of an active navigation aid such as a transponder field or CN3 UUV, or by passive means such as terrain matching.

4.1.4 Communications and Networking

Communication is required between the vehicle and support platform for transmission of commands and data. Primary issues to be considered when evaluating a mode of communication for a UUV task include available bandwidth, range between source and receiver, detectability, and the network infrastructure required. These are of particular concern for the ISR and the ASW missions when communication is desired without exposing either the sender or receiver to possible hostile interception.

Communications is, for the most part, not a major risk area. History has shown that greater bandwidth will be consumed as fast as it becomes available, but sufficient bandwidth exists to perform missions associated with the Sub-Pillars identified in this plan. Nonetheless, an expansion of bandwidth capability is desired for the more stealthy methods, such as acoustic communications and low-probability of intercept radio frequency (RF) communications.

Communication challenges are also associated with multiple vehicles operating together, such as proposed for the MCM mission. Reliable communication between vehicles working in a network must be established and proven. FORCEnet architectures and standards must be developed for UUVs, taking into account mission requirements and UUV capabilities.

4.1.5 Engagement / Intervention

Engagement and intervention techniques are required for a wide range of sub-pillar missions, particularly those requiring long transits and interaction with targets. The MCM mission requires a neutralization capability and the others might involve the use of non-lethal weapons.

A key technology need is the ability to counter threats to UUVs, such as nets. Nets may be intended as UUV countermeasures, or they may be present as a result of normal fishing activities. Net countermeasures could consist of detection and avoidance technologies or the means to extract the UUV from the net, if entangled. Fishing nets pose a significant threat to UUVs, especially in the littoral regions where UUVs are most likely to operate. Investments should be made in the appropriate mix of underwater net detection sensors and ways to avoid or defeat the nets when they are detected or encountered. Defeating the nets by cutting through them may be preferable to maneuvering to avoid them, since going around nets can significantly increase UUV transit distances, expending limited energy. However, this is a trade-off, since cutting through nets requires additional onboard hardware and power as well.

4.2 Engineering Implementation

Engineering implementation is as important as technology development for success. System Engineering considerations are often driven by the sensors, energy sources, and payloads, as well as logistic concerns. However, size and number of vehicles to be used, overall system costs, and interoperability of systems all need to be considered in developing needed capabilities.

4.2.1 Energy Source Selection

The type of energy source selected for a UUV application is driven primarily by mission requirements for speed and endurance. Long endurance, high hotel or payload power, and high speed are all factors that require increased energy capacity on the UUV. It is important to note that energy source selection cannot be done without consideration to the impact on vehicle design, size, and type. There is no clear-cut choice of energy system that meets all mission needs and all vehicle design constraints. This section seeks to clarify the tradeoffs that are involved in selection of energy sources with regard to vehicle design and use.

Representative choices for UUV energy sources (based on a survey of the capabilities and characteristics of current technologies) are primary or rechargeable lithium batteries for smaller sized vehicles, and power plants (fuel cells or hybrid energy systems) for larger vehicles. The pros and cons of these energy sources for UUV applications are shown in Figure 4-6 below.

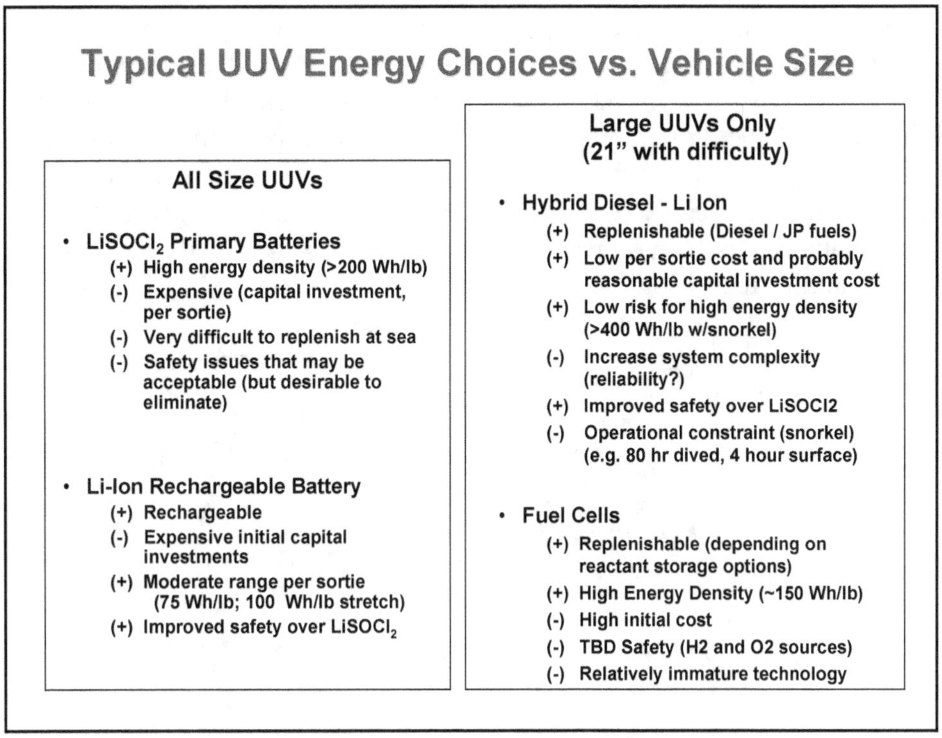

Typical UUV Energy Choices vs. Vehicle Size

All Size UUVs

- **LiSOCl₂ Primary Batteries**
    - (+) High energy density (>200 Wh/lb)
    - (-) Expensive (capital investment, per sortie)
    - (-) Very difficult to replenish at sea
    - (-) Safety issues that may be acceptable (but desirable to eliminate)

- **Li-Ion Rechargeable Battery**
    - (+) Rechargeable
    - (-) Expensive initial capital investments
    - (+) Moderate range per sortie (75 Wh/lb; 100 Wh/lb stretch)
    - (+) Improved safety over LiSOCl₂

Large UUVs Only
(21" with difficulty)

- **Hybrid Diesel - Li Ion**
    - (+) Replenishable (Diesel / JP fuels)
    - (+) Low per sortie cost and probably reasonable capital investment cost
    - (+) Low risk for high energy density (>400 Wh/lb w/snorkel)
    - (-) Increase system complexity (reliability?)
    - (+) Improved safety over LiSOCl2
    - (-) Operational constraint (snorkel) (e.g. 80 hr dived, 4 hour surface)

- **Fuel Cells**
    - (+) Replenishable (depending on reactant storage options)
    - (+) High Energy Density (~150 Wh/lb)
    - (-) High initial cost
    - (-) TBD Safety (H2 and O2 sources)
    - (-) Relatively immature technology

Figure 4-6. UUV Energy Options versus Vehicle Size

Lithium-based batteries, both primary and rechargeable, have the highest energy density among currently available battery technologies. Since these batteries can be packaged from relatively small cells, they are easily configured to fit within most UUV hull shapes, and can provide the energy capacity characteristics required for almost any size or shape UUV. However, there are disadvantages to using primary battery technologies for large energy capacity applications, and for large size vehicles. Specifically, for primary batteries, there is a tremendous cost penalty for applications with large (>500 lbs.) batteries, which are discarded after use. In addition, replenishment (especially at-sea) is a major issue for a UUV that requires rapid reconfigurability. The cost of a primary battery energy section could easily exceed the cost of the UUV itself. Rechargeable batteries are less costly over time. In both cases, the initial capital investments can be quite high both for the batteries, and for support and replenishment equipment. High energy density batteries, such as lithium batteries, also introduce safety concerns, especially on submarines. Rechargeable batteries have a safety advantage since they can be shipped in the discharged state.

For larger size vehicles, fuel cells and hybrid diesel/rechargeable battery power plants become more attractive due to their higher energy density and potentially lower operating costs. Figure 4-7 provides a relative comparison of the various energy options for larger UUVs. For smaller vehicles, these power plants are not an optimal choice; there is a volume penalty due to the need for support equipment to operate the power plant. The energy density of the stored fuel is quite high; but by including the support equipment in the volume allocation, the energy density decreases substantially. This tradeoff is less of a factor as vehicle size increases and the volume available for fuel increases (energy capacity increases). The corresponding volume increase for support equipment is not as great. Overall, the energy capacity grows substantially for larger size UUVs. These power plants have advantages over battery systems. Hybrid diesel power plants are easily replenished. Fuel cells have shorter lives and must eventually be refurbished. Hybrid diesels have the disadvantage of requiring air (periodically surfacing to recharge for several hours). Fuel cells have the advantage of being closed cycle; they can operate continuously until all on-board fuel is consumed. The overall energy capacity for hybrid diesel power plants is vastly superior to present fuel cell technology. Lastly, hybrid diesel is an available technology, low risk, and low cost. Fuel cell technology cost is still quite high; however, its cost should decrease over time.

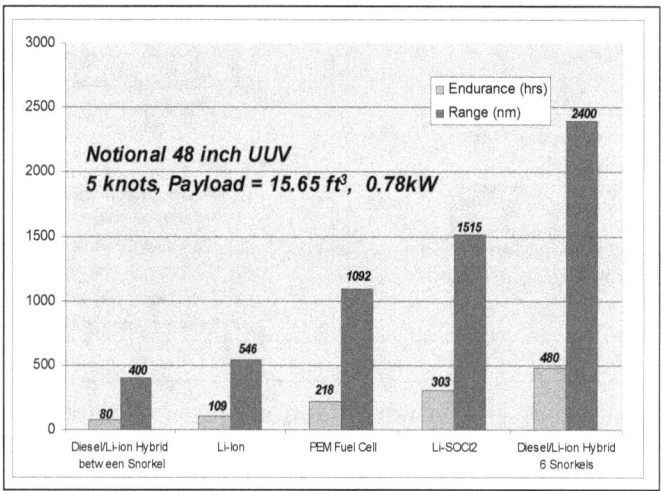

Figure 4-7. Comparison of Large UUV Energy Option Performance

4.2.2 Launch and Recovery

Launch and Recovery (L&R) is a key feature of any UUV system and it is closely related to the vehicle size and host platform characteristics. L&R of large vehicles on a submarine may actually be simpler than with 21-inch vehicles since clearances and alignment may be less restrictive than they are for 21-inch inch diameter vehicles and 21-inch diameter tubes. Although the engineering implications may be simplified, there will be a significant cost associated with submarine platform modifications of this scale. Submarine compatible larger vehicles in the near-term must be either wet docked, towed, or compatible with existing interfaces (missile tubes, dry deck shelters).

Launch and recovery of a large (10-ton) vehicle from a surface craft is a significant engineering challenge. Operation in higher sea states, with or without divers would be difficult, but not insurmountable. This is done on a routine basis in the commercial sector. Cruiser/Destroyer type platforms may be the least capable of taking on such a task, but have the advantages of usually operating forward and having relatively low freeboard. Large deck ships (carriers, amphibious ships and auxiliaries) are either not well suited for the task, have no room in well decks (amphibious ships) or are not always operating forward (auxiliaries). As a result, surface launched and recovered UUVs may have to be engineered to meet the needs of smaller combatants (e.g., Littoral Combat Ship (LCS)), which means that size must be minimized, and 10-ton vehicles may be unacceptably large. In some cases, it may be necessary to use UUVs that are shorter and lighter with subsequent reductions in endurance or payload, to accommodate surface ship handling requirements.

4.2.3   Shipboard Certification of UUV Systems

Ship deployed UUV systems must meet very stringent requirements to be authorized for submarine installation, including, but not limited to, shock requirements, battery (or other energy source) certification, and implodable volume requirements. A similar, but less extensive set of requirements also exists for surface ship certification. Obtaining these certifications can result in significant costs and delays in deploying these systems. Investments should be made early to determine how UUV systems could be designed and built to cost effectively meet ship certification requirements.

4.2.4   Simulation and Visualization

Modeling and simulation are needed for UUV mission planning and reconstruction, vehicle testing, software design and testing, and training. For example, a close link to a robust, real-time environmental analysis (REA) and forecast, and four-dimensional environment is essential if we are to create optimal UUV sortie plans that account for environmental effects, provide needed safety margins, and allow for more accurate mission reconstruction.

4.3   UUV Interoperability and Connectivity

One of the key features of UUV systems in the future will be the interconnectivity and interoperability provided via FORCEnet (Figure 4-8). As stated in Sea Power 21, "FORCEnet is the operational construct and architectural framework for naval warfare in the Information Age which integrates warriors, sensors, networks, command and control, platforms and weapons, into a networked, distributed combat force, scaleable across the spectrum of conflict from seabed to space and sea to land." It is an inherently joint and coalition concept, both relying on and providing essential capabilities to the joint and coalition communities and other services and agencies. By being FORCEnet compliant, a UUV system will ensure that its data product is delivered to the proper operating systems and via established communication paths, allowing the most effective use and dissemination to warfighters.

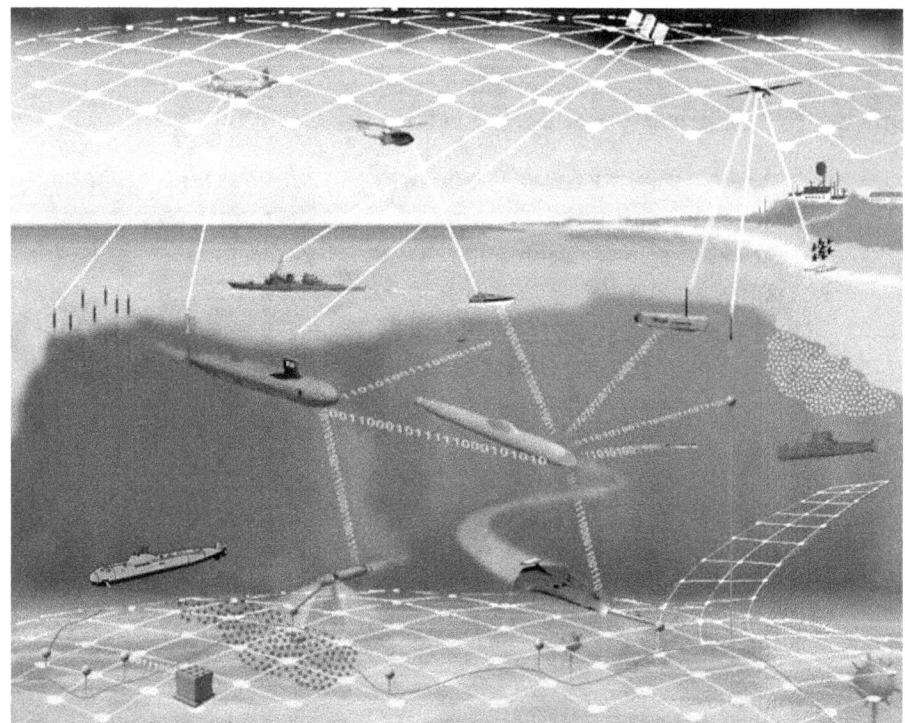

Figure 4-8. FORCEnet in Action

4.3.1 FORCEnet Compatibility

While all Fleet UUV systems will be FORCEnet compliant in the future, the degree and type of integration will be driven by mission requirements. As part of the UUV system design, the Information Exchange Requirements (IER) and C3 (Command, Control, and Communication) Assessment Matrices will be developed, defining the information and communication interfaces required. With a network-based architecture, a UUV and its sensors may be configured as a node on the information network, allowing connection with the communities of interest.

To ensure interoperability, the FORCEnet Compliance Checklist provides references for the following critical areas as well as the DoD Joint Technical Architecture. Many of these requirements are the commonly accepted industry standards, and the use of open architectures permits the greatest flexibility and interoperability possible. The checklist includes:

- FORCEnet Operational Requirements
- FORCEnet System / Technical Requirements
- FORCEnet Support / Policy Requirements
- FORCEnet Implementation Requirements
- Architecture and Standards
- Human Systems Integration
- Spectrum Management
- Information Assurance
- Joint Interoperability

4.3.2 Implementation Strategy

FORCEnet is a spiral development, evolving to meet the needs of the Fleet and joint and coalition forces. The UUV community of developers, users and resource sponsors will be an active part of this process ensuring that the specific needs and benefits of unmanned systems are addressed within the developing architectures and standards.

The user community will identify and define the data products of the UUV systems under development, and also identify the users of those data products. As that is accomplished for each system, the appropriate standards and formats will be determined to ensure the proper dissemination of the products. Similarly, the appropriate communication requirements for each system will be defined, and the available communication channels and capacity identified.

The UUV community must participate in the groups developing FORCEnet standards and architectures relevant to UUV operations to ensure that UUV specific needs are met. The Undersea FORCEnet Process Implementation Working Group *[Outbrief March 5, 2004]* has begun to identify the needs of the undersea community, many of which are relevant to UUV integration. Key among these is the recommendation to establish standards for the following areas:

- Acoustic communications (including LPI waveforms)
- RF (SATCOM and line of sight) communications in compliance with the DoD Joint Technical Architecture and FORCEnet architecture
- Optical communications (underwater and air-water interface)
- Information Security (INFOSEC)
- Information exchange standards for processed and unprocessed data (supporting a range of data processing and fusion architectures from sharing raw sensor data, beam-formed data, track data and snippets, track data only)
- Allied and Coalition connectivity and data exchange

In addition to the development of standards and architectures, the UUV community will participate in the various pilot programs developing and demonstrating implementation methods for FORCEnet integration for undersea systems. Experimentation with the systems within the Fleet operational environment will provide valuable data regarding the best means of designing and implementing the necessary architectures and systems.

5 Recommendations and Conclusions

A number of recommendations are made for the development plan of UUV programs. These include the formation of four general vehicle classes, recommendations for technology development, and increased involvement with Fleet experimentation. The overall goal is:

Deliver UUV Capability...and Begin Using It!

5.1 Meeting Mission Requirements with Four Classes of UUVs

Meeting mission requirements and minimizing cost are the two major considerations that must be addressed when developing UUV acquisition programs. Among the nine Sub-Pillar UUV missions that were identified, there is significant commonality among UUV functions. In some cases, commonality is driven by external influences, such as platform interfaces (e.g., handling equipment, communications). Given these facts, it does not make economic sense to build "nine vehicles to perform nine missions." To help minimize the cost of future UUV systems, it is beneficial to maximize commonality among UUV systems (e.g., sharing vehicle components, equipment and assets). For the larger size vehicles (12.75 inches in diameter and up), significant efficiencies can be realized by focusing developments toward standard vehicle sizes.

The span of the Sub-Pillar capabilities can be met with vehicles ranging in size from man-portable to large size. Platform interfaces, existing infrastructure, and the spectrum of mission requirements lead us to four vehicle classes:

- Man-Portable,
- Light Weight Vehicle (LWV),
- Heavy Weight Vehicle (HWV), and
- Large Class

with nominal level of performance in accordance with Figure 5-1.

Class	Diameter (inches)	Displacement (lbs.)	Endurance High Hotel Load (hours)	Endurance Low Hotel Load (hours)	Payload (ft^3)
Man-Portable	3 - 9	< 100	< 10	10 - 20	< 0.25
LWV	12.75	~ 500	10 - 20	20 - 40	1 - 3
HWV	21	< 3,000	20 - 50	40 - 80	4 - 6
Large	> 36	~ 20,000	100 - 300	>> 400	15 - 30 + External Stores

Figure 5-1. UUV Classes

The Sub-Pillar capabilities of Chapter 3 were then mapped to the vehicle classes, resulting in the summary shown in Figure 5-2.

Seapower Pillar	Priority	Sub Pillar Capability	Man Portable	LWV	HWV	Large
FORCEnet	1	Intelligence, Surveillance, Reconnaissance	Special Purpose	Harbor	Tactical	Persistent
FORCEnet	5	Oceanography		Special Purpose	Littoral Access	Long Range
FORCEnet	6	Communication / Navigation Network Nodes	VSW / SOF	Mobile CN3		
Sea Shield	2	Mine Countermeasures	VSW / SW SCM / RI Neutralizers	OPAREA Clearance	Clandestine Recon.	
Sea Shield	3	Anti-Submarine Warfare				Hold-at-Risk
Sea Shield	4	Inspection / ID	HLD/ATFP			
Sea Base	7	Payload Delivery				SOF, ASW, MCM, TCS**
Sea Strike	8	Information Operations		Network Attack	Submarine Decoy	
Sea Strike	9	Time Critical Strike				(see Payload Delivery)

Figure 5-2. UUV Class vs. Mission

The next sections discuss the rationale for the typical missions and characteristics of the four vehicle classes.

5.1.1   Man Portable Vehicle Class

Man portable UUVs are appropriately named due to their small sizes and weights. The vehicles can be deployed from most platforms or shore sites, but are typically deployed by a few men in rubber boats. The displacement of these vehicles is generally up to 100 pounds (two-man lift). Size and shape are open issues for this class; they are driven by program needs and requirements. This class of vehicles supports the Sub-Pillar capabilities in the following areas:

- Special Purpose ISR
- Expendable CN3
- Very Shallow Water (VSW) / SW MCM (Coastal / Riverine)
- MCM Neutralizer
- Inspect / ID
- Explosive Ordnance Disposal (EOD)

5.1.2   Light Weight Vehicle (LWV) Class

Light Weight Vehicles are next up in size and weight from Man-Portable UUVs. The vehicle size is defined as nominally 12.75-inches in diameter, and will typically be cylindrically shaped vehicles. This size fills the need for a vehicle with extended endurance and is still relatively easily handled. Existing 12.75-inch diameter vehicle (Lightweight Torpedo) hardware, handling equipment, launchers, and recovery equipment can be leveraged. This size is also the largest that is easily supported by existing USVs or aircraft. This class of vehicles supports the Sub-Pillar capabilities in the following areas:

- Harbor ISR
- Special Oceanography
- Mobile CN3
- Network Attack (IO)
- MCM OPAREA Reconnaissance

5.1.3 Heavy Weight Vehicle (HWV) Class

Heavy Weight Vehicles are nominally 21 inches in diameter, including UUVs that are submarine torpedo tube compatible. HWVs are typically cylindrical shaped. This class of vehicles supports Sub-Pillar capabilities in the following areas:

- Tactical ISR
- Oceanography
- MCM Clandestine Reconnaissance
- Submarine Decoy

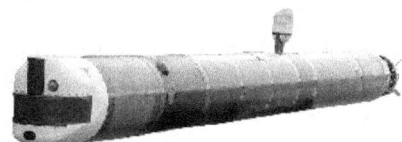

5.1.4 Large Vehicle Class

This vehicle class will be the largest size vehicles to be operated. The driving factor for the large size is endurance and payload capacity. In order to travel long distances (>100 miles), and to have long times on station (>1 week), their energy capacity must be significant. As discussed in Chapter 4, energy sources such as fuel cells and hybrid diesel/rechargeable batteries can provide adequate energy capacity.

Standardization of modules is particularly desirable in this class of vehicles. In addition to existing UUV standards that specify electrical, communications, and computer interfaces, it will be necessary to define mechanical interfaces for the Large Class of vehicles. It is possible that external pods could be added for additional fuel, to carry deployable payloads, etc. The vehicle length could be selectable based on mission requirements, size of payload, and platform interface. It is anticipated that the upper limit on the Large Vehicle Class cross-section would be 72 inches, based on vertical launch tube constraints. Slightly smaller cross-sections would allow the use of external pods, providing greater flexibility and ease of replenishment. This class of vehicles supports the Sub-Pillar capabilities in the following areas:

- Persistent ISR
- ASW Hold at Risk
- Long Range Oceanography (future)
- Payload Delivery (MIW, ASW, SOF, EOD, TCS)

5.2 Commonality and Modularity of UUVs

In order to provide cost-effective and flexible capabilities, programs should strive to maximize commonality and modularity of UUV systems, as a minimum within a given class. UUV programs must adopt standards and design for open architecture whenever practicable. Some initial guidance on common interfaces is provided in the Draft UUV Standards Study of 2003, and FORCEnet architecture and standards. Use of common core subsystems (e.g., computer systems, sensors, navigation systems, and communications) should be implemented to the maximum extent possible. Although certain core systems will be common within a class of UUVs, there will most certainly be 'flavors' of UUVs within a class, particularly in the smaller vehicles. A pertinent example is the Man-Portable class, where a variety of specific UUVs will exist to meet a wide range of mission requirements. Larger sized UUVs, particularly HWV and Large Vehicle classes, should be increasingly modular. The Large Vehicle Class should be fully modular to accommodate varying configurations of payloads and platform interfaces.

5.3 Programmatic Recommendations

Through analysis of the fleet needs, available technology, and expected advancements, the following broad programmatic recommendations are made:

- Develop Four UUV Classes
- Develop Standards and Implement Modularity
- Maintain a Balanced UUV Technology Program
- Increase Experimentation in UUV Technology
- Coordinate with Other Unmanned Vehicle Programs
- Field Systems in the Fleet

5.3.1 Develop Four UUV Classes

To address the nine Sea Power 21 Sub-Pillar capabilities, this document recommends evolving towards four vehicle classes. This will be achieved with integration of current and future UUV programs. In the long term, this evolution will lead to efficiencies in handling systems, other platform interfaces, and interchange of payloads. Varied configurations or "flavors" are expected within each class. For example, the Man-Portable class includes gliders, hovering vehicles, and Fleet fielded Semi-Autonomous Hydrographic Reconnaissance Vehicle (SAHRV) and SCULPIN systems. The roadmap of Figure 5-2 illustrates how existing UUV efforts will evolve to four vehicle classes. Some capabilities have already been fielded and others are in the late stages of Test and Evaluation. Lightweight and large vehicle efforts are advanced in the commercial world, and are being leveraged to serve Fleet requirements.

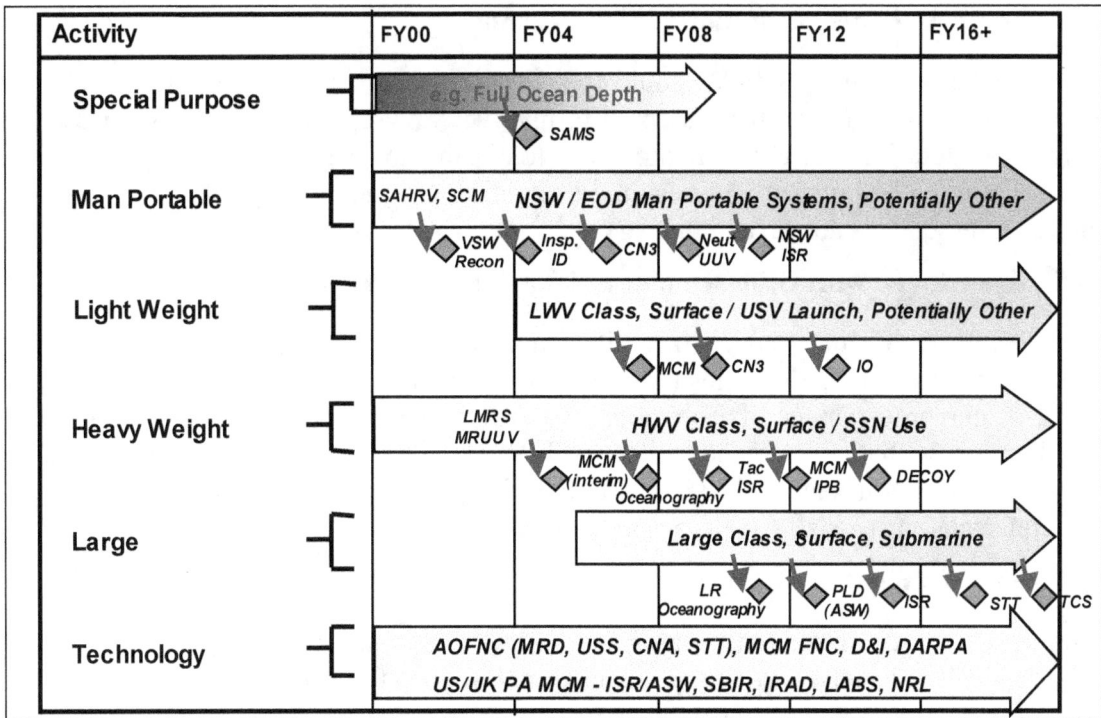

Figure 5-3. UUV Master Plan Program Roadmap

5.3.2 Develop Standards and Implement Modularity

The programmatic recommendation to continue to develop standards for UUVs will ease interchangeability of modules. By developing and following up-to-date standard interfaces, the need for custom interfaces is mitigated or eliminated. Use of Commercial-Off-the-Shelf (COTS) equipment will drive acceptance of current commercial practice and standards. Use of Navy and DoD standards such as FORCEnet based architectures will ensure UUV interoperability with other systems.

Standardization will also facilitate the implementation of UUV modularity. Many core UUV functional components may be shared within and across vehicle classes, including: payloads, navigation, energy, communications, some sensors, and launch and recovery systems. The ability to adapt hardware and software from one vehicle class to another will cut cost and time to employment. Vehicle configurations should be designed to ease configuration changes, such as adding new payloads. This is especially true for the larger two classes of UUVs, as custom interfaces will be prohibitively expensive. Maximization of sharing within a class (or even to other classes) not only provides a benefit during acquisition, but also during the life cycles of systems.

5.3.3 Maintain a Balanced UUV Technology Program

A balanced technology program for both UUV payloads and platforms is required to support the nine capabilities described in this document. Specific technology recommendations and roadmaps are described in Section 5.3.7.

5.3.4   Increase Experimentation in UUV Technology

Experimentation with systems should be expanded to provide risk reduction for technology and operations. It is essential to involve Navy operators through outreach to operational, doctrine, and training commands to expand and refine employment concepts. Innovation must be pursued with test and evaluation programs using UUV technologies from government, academia, and industry.

5.3.5   Coordinate with Other Unmanned Vehicle Programs

While there are obvious and distinct differences between requirements for UUVs and other types of unmanned vehicles (e.g., energy, navigation, and communications), there are also numerous areas of commonality (e.g., autonomy and mission planning). Coordination with the developers of the USV Master Plan and Unmanned Systems Strategic Plan (USSP), as well as interaction at the technical level, can provide synergies and reduce costs across all the Navy's unmanned vehicle programs.

5.3.6   Field Systems in the Fleet

Continued introduction of functional UUVs into the fleet is critical. Fleet sailors have enthusiastically received a variety of small vehicles since the approval of the last Master Plan. Fleet fielded systems such as SAHRV (NSW) and SCULPIN (EOD) not only provided operational capabilities in contingencies such as Operation Iraqi Freedom, but also provide a critical pool of educated Fleet UUV operators who are a critical link in the evolution of future generations of UUVs. Execution of larger vehicle programs needs to be in accordance with a "spiral development" philosophy. Some capabilities, even if they are interim, need to be provided to the fleet as soon as possible. ***A partial technical solution in-use in the Fleet is worth more than perfection in the laboratory.***

5.3.7   Human Systems Integration (HSI)

The product of UUV use is knowledge and data to the warfighter today, and in the future direct actions which aid the warfighter. As a result, the integration of the unmanned system with the "manned" system is paramount. HSI should be addressed as a major part of every UUV program and exercise. A comprehensive strategy for HSI will encompass all of the seven domains: Human Factors Engineering; Personnel; Habitability; Manpower; Training; Environment, Safety and Health; and Survivability. Addressing these factors will be the dominant challenge in the fielding of low cost / COTS UUV systems.

The goal of UUV Program HSI efforts, in conjunction with the NAVSEA HSI Directorate, is to deliver well-engineered and usable systems for Warfighters. Through coordinated and cooperative application of HSI principles, the UUV Programs will meet these objectives, improve Fleet training and readiness, enhance Sailor performance and professional development, and reduce life cycle costs.

5.4   Technical Recommendations

This study noted the excellent progress of the R&D community in meeting many of the technical recommendations of the last UUV Master Plan. Based on the technical assessment discussed in Chapter 4 of this document, the following investments in critical technologies are recommended:

- Autonomy
- Energy and Propulsion
- Sensors and Sensor Processing
- Communications / Networking
- Engagement / Intervention

5.4.1 Autonomy

The technology readiness analysis (Section 4.1) indicated a deficiency in autonomy readiness across all functions. Autonomy is needed to support long, complex missions in unpredictable or harsh environments. It includes the need to make independent decisions, based on the mission goals, environmental conditions, and remaining energy on-board. Additional needed capabilities include the need to avoid obstacles and entanglements, to react to changes in ambient conditions, and to engage in group behavior when multiple UUVs are needed to act as a team. Figure 5-4 is a recommended roadmap for future autonomy development.

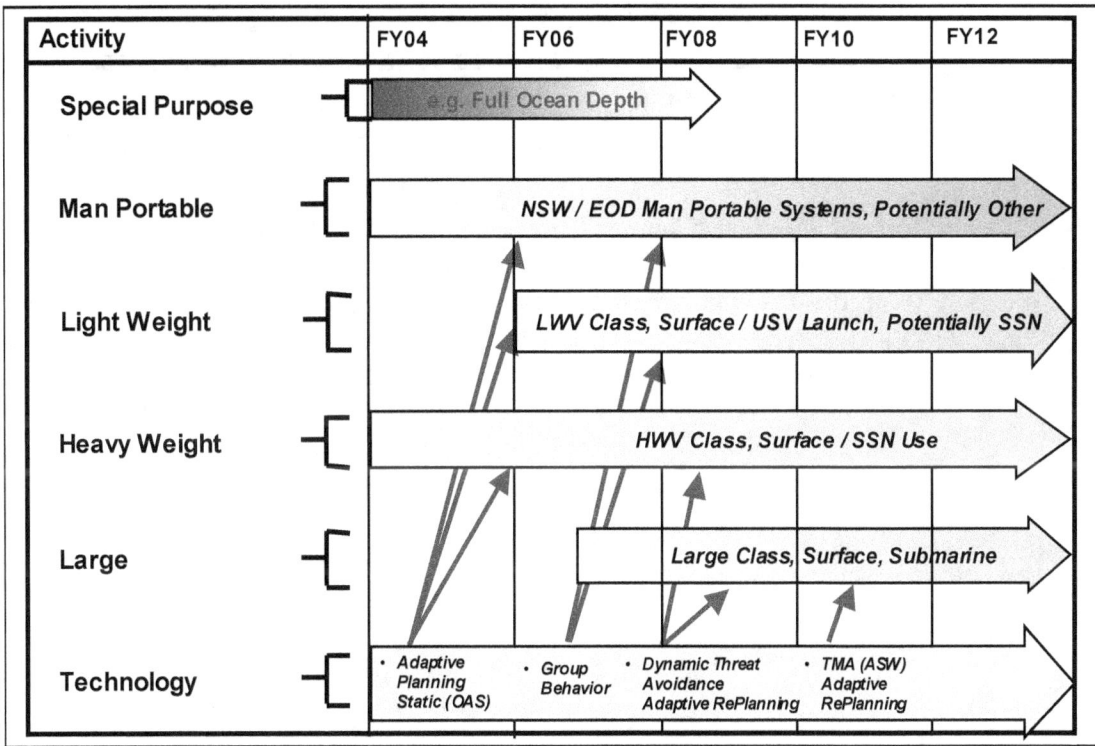

Figure 5-4. Technology Roadmap for Autonomy

5.4.2 Energy and Propulsion

Low-cost, high energy density, reliable, safe, long-duration easily recharged or refueled power sources are needed in all Sub-Pillar capabilities. Advanced energy and propulsion, in combination with other UUV technologies, will enable the use of smaller vehicles (reducing cost) in the long term, and will provide greater performance. Figure 5-5 is a recommended roadmap for future energy developments.

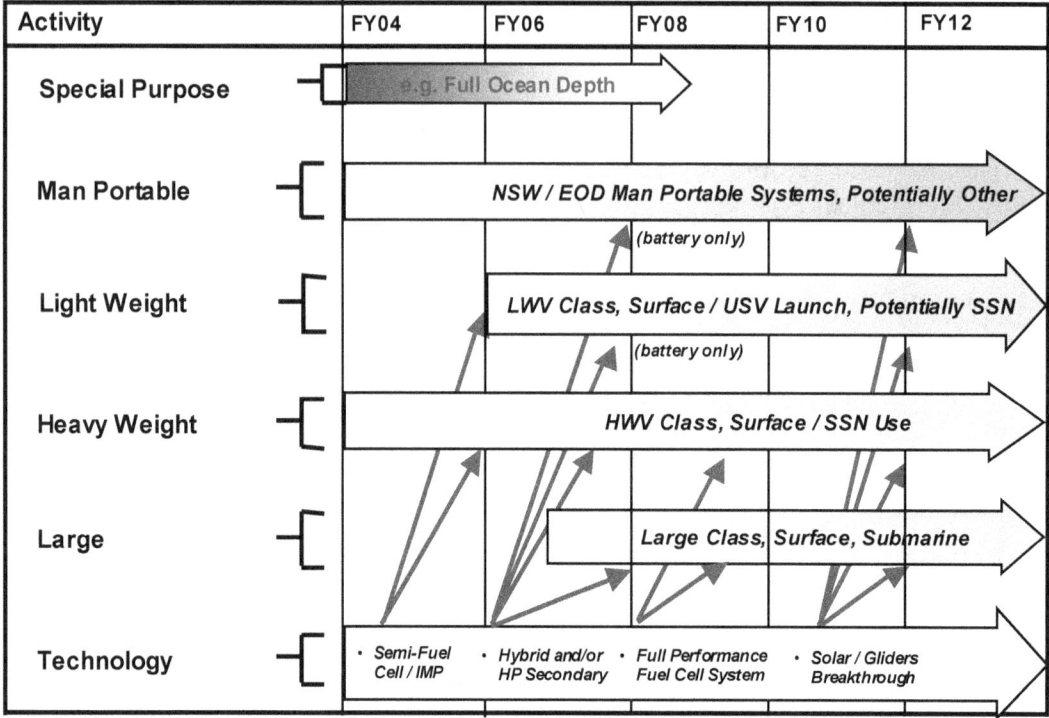

Figure 5-5. Technology Roadmap for Energy

5.4.3   Sensors and Sensor Processing

While sensor technology is at a higher Technology Readiness Level (TRL) for some missions and functions, continued investment in automatic target classification and identification is needed.   Other areas of sensor development include Non-Traditional Tracking (NTT) sensors for ASW, novel sensors for CBNRE and compact ISR. Figure 5-6 is a recommended roadmap for future sensor developments.

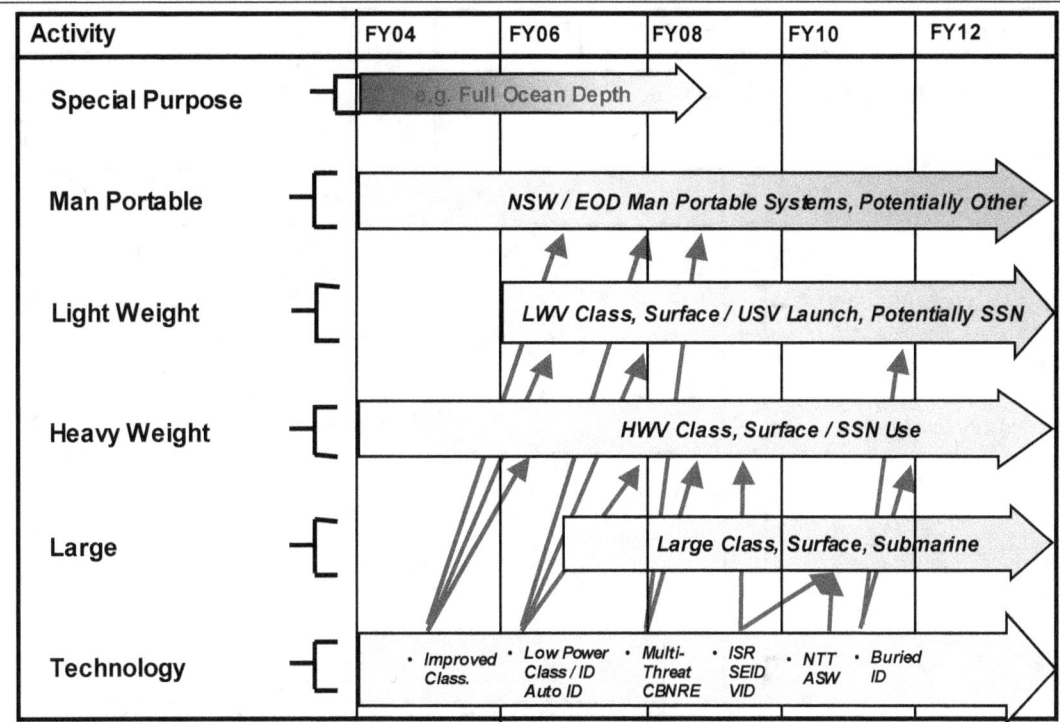

Figure 5-6. Technology Roadmap for Sensors

5.4.4 Communications / Networking

Investment and realistic testing are needed to ensure that UUVs can transmit RF data reliably in operational sea states. Real-time or near-real-time RF communications are needed for missions such as tactical ISR. RF communications from a UUV to a host platform presents a challenge due to limited mast height and poor stability while operating on or near the surface. Investment is needed in acoustic or other (e.g., laser) underwater communications technologies. Communications at useful data rates while maintaining vehicle speed and depth remain a challenge for both submarines and UUVs. Figure 5-7 is a recommended roadmap for future communications developments.

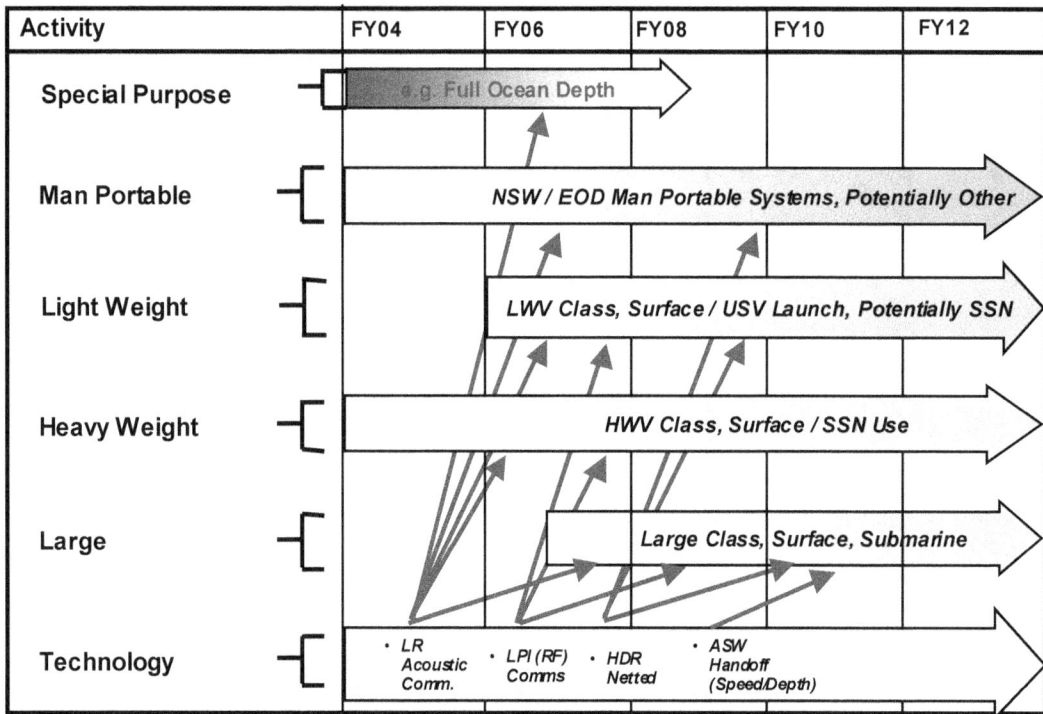

Figure 5-7. Technology Roadmap for Communications/Networking

5.4.5 Engagement / Intervention

Development of technology is needed to support net extraction, autonomous neutralizers for MCM missions, and non-lethal weapons (NLW) for ASW and Inspection / Identification missions. Figure 5-8 is a recommended roadmap for future engagement and intervention developments.

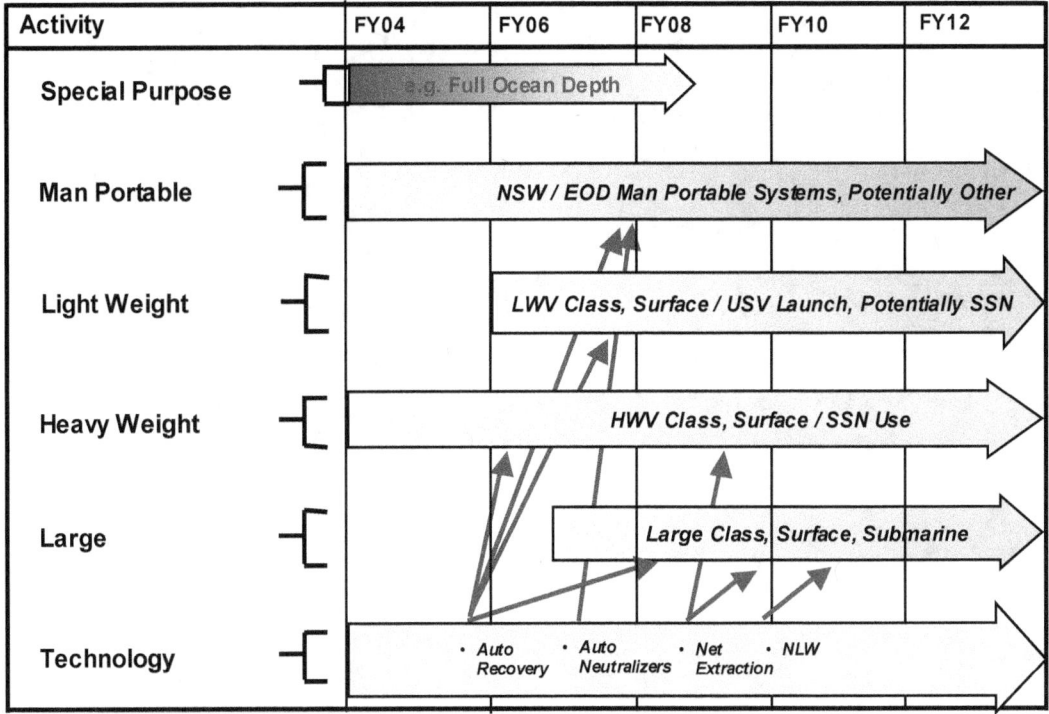

Figure 5-8. Technology Roadmap for Engagement Intervention

5.5 Conclusion

The goal of the Master Plan is to provide a strategy to rapidly deliver new UUV capabilities to the Fleet, with a strategy for upgrading those capabilities with minimal time and expense. This plan effectively synergizes the efforts under legacy, developmental, and technology programs. Development and fielding of advanced technologies will provide growth and dominance. The establishment of standards will be critical to the success of future systems, for without them the required modularity will not be achieved. The effective introduction of UUVs into the Fleet will significantly contribute to the Navy's control of the maritime battlespace.

Deliver UUV Capability…and Begin Using It

Appendix A: References

Eleventh International Symposium on Unmanned Untethered Submersible Technology, 1999. Autonomous Undersea Systems Institute, Lee, NH.

European Mine Countermeasures Technology: A Survey and Assessment, 1993. Lobb, R. Kenneth, Office of Naval Research European Office, 12 January 1993, Arlington, VA.

IHO Standards for Hydrographic Surveys, 4th Ed., April 1998, Special Publication No. 44, International Hydrographic Bureau, Monaco.

Jane's Underwater Technology First Edition 1998-99, 1998. Clifford Funnell, editor, Jane's Information Group Limited, Surrey, UK.

Naval Doctrine Publication 1, Office of the Chief of Naval Operations.

Department of the Navy 1999 Posture Statement, Office of the Chief of Naval Operations

Forward...From the Sea, The Navy Operational Concept, Office of the Chief of Naval Operations, March 1997.

Navy UUV Master Plan- Presentation to the Oversight Board, 26 July 1999. Paul M. Dunn, presenter. Naval Undersea Warfare Center, RI.

Oceans '99 MTS/IEEE Conference Proceedings, 1999. Marine Technology Society, Washington, D.C.

Operational Effectiveness of Unmanned Underwater Systems, 1999. Robert L. Wernli, editor, Marine Technology Society, Washington, D.C.

Remotely Operated Vehicles of the World '98/9 Edition, 1998. Oilfield Publications Limited, Houston TX.

ROV Review 1993-1994 5th Edition, 1993. Windate Enterprises, San Diego, CA.

Technology and the Mine Problem Symposium Proceedings, 1996. Naval Postgraduate School, Monterey, CA.

Third International Symposium on Technology and the Mine Problem Proceedings, 1998. Naval Postgraduate School, Monterey, CA.

Underwater Intervention 1999 Conference Proceedings, 1999. Association of Diving Contractors, Marine Technology Society, Washington, D.C.

Undersea Vehicles and National Needs, 1996. Marine Board Commission on Engineering and Technical Systems, National Research Council, National Academy Press, Washington, D.C.

Unmanned Vehicles in Mine Countermeasures, 1999. Naval Research Advisory Committee, Washington, D.C.

"Sea Strike: Projecting Persistent Responsive, and Precise Power," Naval Institute Proceedings, December 2002.

"A Future Naval Capability, Time Critical Strike," Office of Naval Research, www.onr.navy.mil, April 2004.

"Forward Pass, Vignette 5: Time Critical Strike," Defense Advanced Research Projects Agency, October 10, 2000.

The Navy Unmanned Undersea Vehicle (UUV) Master Plan, Assistant Secretary of the Navy for Research Development & Acquisition, April 20, 2000.

Small UUV Strategic Plan , Program Executive Officer for Mine and Undersea Warfare, 28 June 2002.

Analysis of Alternatives (AoA) for Large Displacement UUVs (LD MR UUV) Study, 2004.

Unmanned Undersea Vehicles: 2010 and Beyond (Final Report), Naval War College, Newport, RI, 30 November 2003.

Explosive Ordnance Disposal (EOD) Anti-Terrorism / Force Protection (AT/FP) Unmanned Underwater Vehicle (UUV) Mission Requirement Priorities, Commander Explosive Ordnance Disposal Group TWO ltr 8027 Ser. N8/145 dtd Jun 13, 2003.

Projecting Decisive Joint Capabilities, Naval Instititue *Proceedings*, October 2002, ADM Vern Clark, USN.

Sea Shield: Projecting Global Defensive Assurance, Naval Instititue *Proceedings*, November 2002, VADM Mike Bucchi,, USN, and VADM Mike Mullen, USN.

Sea Strike: Projecting Persistent, Responsive, and Precise Power, Naval Instititue *Proceedings*, December 2002, VADM Cutler Dawson, USN, and VADM John Nathman, USN.

Sea Basing: Operational Independence for a New Century, Naval Instititue *Proceedings*, January 2003, VADM Charles W. Moore Jr., USN, and Lt. Gen. Edward Hanlon Jr., USMC.

ForceNet: Turning Information into Power, Naval Instititue *Proceedings*, February 2003, VADM Richard W. Mayo, USN, and VADM John Nathman, USN.

Unmanned Aerial Vehicles (UAV) Roadmap 2002-2027, Office of the Secretary of Defense, December 2002

Joint Robotics Program Master Plan FY2002, Undersecretary of Defense for Acquisition, Technology, & Logistics, Strategic and Tactical Systems, 2002.

Naval Readiness Augmentation: A Concept for Unmanned Systems in the Navy, Science, Technology, Analysis and Special Operations Department, Coastal Systems Station, Code R10, June 2001.

FORCEnet Architecture and Standards, November 2003.

Roles of Unmanned Vehicles, Naval Research Advisory Committee (NRAC), March 2002.

Navy Strategic Plan for Small Unmanned Underwater Vehicles, June 2002.

Contested Submarine Mission Area CONOPS Study, Office of Naval Research (Office of Naval Research).

Organic Mine Countermeasures End-to-End Assessment.

Task Force ASW Report, 2004.

Fletcher, B.E., *Physical Security Applications for ROV Technology*. Presented at Intervention '90, Vancouver, BC, 06/27/90. Published in Conference Proceedings, June, 1990, 08/02/90.

National Military Strategy of the United States of America 2004, Joint Chiefs of Staff,

FY 2005 Naval Mine Countermeasures Plan (2 March 2004)

Appendix B: Year 2000 UUV Master Plan Field Study Results

Interviews were performed with a large number of potential users in the Fleet, Industry, Science and Academia, and other Federal Agencies. The emphasis was placed on potential users of UUVs, as opposed to those solely involved with the technology development. While some potential users were not interviewed due to time and scheduling constraints, the broad cross section of interviewers and interviewees provided a full range of UUV applications.

Navy and Marine Corps Applications

From the fleet perspective, a great deal of interest was expressed in various aspects of mine countermeasures, both in realizing those missions outlined in the 1994 plan and as a continuing expansion of the work currently being performed. Other high priority missions from the Naval perspective included intelligence / surveillance / reconnaissance (ISR), anti-submarine warfare (ASW), undersea search and survey, and tactical oceanography.

Table B-1: Navy and Marine Corps Potential Users and Associated Applications

Source	Primary UUV Interests
CNO N84T: ASW Division	ISR, Tactical Ocean., Offense and Defense
CNO N852: Mine Warfare Branch, Expeditionary Warfare Division	MCM for AOA
CNO N863B: Maritime Warfare Branch, Surface Warfare Division	ASW, MCM, Tactical Oceanography
CNO N873B: Deep Submergence Branch, Submarine Warfare Division	MCM, Surveillance, Tactical Ocean.
CNO N875: Science and Technology Branch, Submarine Warfare Division	ISR, ASW
CNO N88: Air Warfare Division	Surveillance, MIW, Battlespace Dominance
CINCLANT: Commander in Chief, Atlantic	MCM—All depths
COMINEWARCOM: Mine Warfare Command	MCM—All depths
NAVOCEANO: Naval Oceanographic Office	Tactical Oceanography
PEO-MIW-EOD: Mine Warfare – Explosive Ordnance Disposal	VSW-SW MCM
SUBDEVRON5: Submarine Development Squadron	Search and recovery
SWDG Surface Warfare Development Group	MCM including beach zone
USACOM US Atlantic Command	ISR, Comms, Tactical Ocean., Target ID

(note: became US Joint Forces Command 7 Oct 99)	
USCENTCOM US Central Command	Reconnaissance, Bathymetry, MCM
USSOCOM US Special Operations Command	VSW MCM

Commercial Applications

UUVs are becoming more widely accepted in industry, as the technology matures and systems become a cost-effective alternative to conventional methods. This is particularly true in the offshore oil and gas domain, where the need to operate in deeper water requires the use of advanced technologies. This includes long-range surveys for cable and pipelaying and subsea intervention and operations. Other commercial areas where vehicles are playing a greater role include automated ship hull inspection, infrastructure inspection, and operations in hazardous environments. UUVs have become commercially viable and accepted, as evidenced by the Norwegian HUGIN vehicle, the Danish Martin, and the English Autosub, all currently in regular operation.

Table B-2: Commercial Potential Users and Associated Applications

Source	Primary UUV Interests
American Bureau of Shipping	Ship hull inspection
C&C Technologies	Bathymetric survey
Cybernetix	Subsea oil and gas intervention
Deep Ocean Engineering	Infrastructure and nuclear Inspection, subsea intervention
Imetrix	Ship hull inspection, infrastructure inspection, aquaculture
International Submarine Engineering	Bathymetric survey, cable laying, mine countermeasures
Norwesco	Infrastructure inspection
Oceaneering	Subsea oil and gas intervention
Shell	Subsea oil and gas intervention
Simrad	Bathymetric survey

Science and Academic Applications

Much of the UUV development has occurred in academic circles, both for scientific and military applications. In many of these cases, the scientific needs have driven the development of the technologies required to perform the mission. These include bathymetric mapping and deep-water sampling. In other cases, the technologies are only now beginning to reach a point whereby the missions can be realized, especially where long-term operation is required.

Table B-3: Science and Academic Potential Users and Associated Applications

Source	Primary UUV Interests
Naval Postgraduate School	Mine countermeasures, advanced control applications
Naval Research Laboratory: Mapping Charting & Geodesy Branch	Bathymetric charting
Scripps Institute of Oceanography	Long term bottom monitoring, biological sampling, water sampling, current mapping
Texas A&M University	Geophysical Survey
University of Rhode Island	Rapid Environmental Assessment, Focused Environmental Assessment
University of South Florida	Micro data following
University of Washington: Applied Physics Laboratory	Long term, long range oceanographic monitoring
Woods Hole Oceanographic Institution	Integrated autonomous systems

Other Government Users

Other government agencies have also evidenced a need for UUV type operations. These include a full range of applications from hazardous waste operations for the Department of Energy, to fisheries research for NOAA, to drug interdiction by the Coast Guard to bathymetric mapping for the USGS. Recent events off the coast of New England also point to an occasional need for object search and recovery by the National Transportation Safety Board and Federal Aviation Agency.

Table B-4: Other Government Potential Users and Associated Applications

Source	Primary UUV Interests
Defense Special Weapons Agency	Underwater security
Department of Energy	Hazardous material handling
National Oceanographic & Atmospheric Administration	Fisheries research
Office of Naval Research	Synoptic Ocean Observation, MCM
US Coast Guard	Damage assessment, drug interdiction
US Geologic Survey	Bathymetric mapping

Appendix C: Year 2000 UUV Master Plan Expert Panels

Core Study Team for year 2000 Navy UUV Master Plan:

The Core Team developing the plan was a group of UUV experts from a range of Navy laboratories and academia. Team members have extensive experience in UUV applications for mine countermeasures, anti-submarine warfare and training, search and salvage, tactical oceanography, surveillance, inspection, and undersea work.

Paul Dunn, Study Technical Director, Naval Undersea Warfare Center, Newport
Dave DeMartino, Naval Surface Warfare Center, Panama City
Robert Wernli, Space and Naval Warfare Systems Center, San Diego
Barbara Fletcher, Space and Naval Warfare Systems Center, San Diego
Joe Hanlin, CNO N0943H
Carey Ingram, Naval Meteorology and Oceanographic Command
Martha Head, Naval Meteorology and Oceanographic Command
Pat Madden, Johns Hopkins University Applied Physics Laboratory

Core Team Advisors

In addition to the Core Team, and separate from the Innovation Workshop participants listed below, several people experienced in the UUV field provided input to the UUV Master Plan. These advisors to the core team included:

J. Brad Mooney, RADM, USN (Ret.)
CAPT John Polcari, DARPA
Tom Curtin, Office of Naval Research
Mack O'Brien, Charles Stark Draper Laboratory
Lt Larry Estrada, SUBDEVRONFIVE

Oversight Board

Stakeholders in UUV development were represented by the Oversight Board, chaired by the Assistant Secretary of the Navy (Research, Development and Acquisition). They were briefed at regular intervals during preparation of the Master Plan, and provided guidance as to the direction and content. Board members included:

Dr. Lee Buchanan, ASN (RD&A)
Dr. Paris Genalis, USD (A&T) Naval Warfare
Mr. Dale Gerry, DASN (M/UW)
Mr. Tim Douglass, PEO (USW)
RADM Ray Smith, CNO N81
RADM W. Clyde Marsh, CNO N85B
RADM Paul Schultz CNO N86B
RADM Winford Ellis, CNO N873
RADM Paul Gaffney, CNR/CNO N091/USMC Assistant DCOS (S&T)
RADM Charlie Young, NAVSEA 93/COMNaval Undersea Warfare Center
Dr. John Sirmalis, Naval Undersea Warfare Center Technical Director
RADM Ken Barbor, COMNAVMETOCCOM
Mr. Paul Lowell, Deputy DNI

Innovation Workshop

To insure that a full spectrum of innovative concepts was considered, an Innovation Workshop was held on 8 June 1999. Using the Group Systems software at the Navy Acquisition Center of Excellence, a variety of underwater experts brainstormed UUV applications and technologies. Participants included representatives from the Office of Naval Research, independent consultants, industry, and various Navy laboratories.

At the workshop, computer groupware tools were use to solicit and organize ideas and concepts for UUV applications. As a starting point, a list of current critical at-sea tasks was compiled including MCM, ASW, power projection / strike, ISR, logistics, tactical oceanography, force protection, search and rescue, personnel evacuation, inspection, work, and object recovery. Working from these tasks, important breakthrough missions for Navy UUVs were identified and ranked. In priority order, these included: clandestine intelligence gathering, mine countermeasures, power projection, ASW sanitization, combined ASW / MCM mission, truck / delivery device, dual use bathymetric survey, global monitoring of ocean health and status, and replacement of SSNs for littoral operations.

Participants in the Innovation Workshop were:

Jack Bachkosky, Naval Research Advisory Council
Dick Rumpf, RAI
J. Brad Mooney, RADM, USN (Ret.)
Tom Curtin, Office of Naval Research
Henry Gonzalez, former deputy Program Manager PMS 403B
Tom Frank, Naval Undersea Warfare Center
Sam Hester, Naval Undersea Warfare Center
Chris Hillenbrand, Office of Naval Research
David Jourdan, Nauticos
Harvey Ko, Johns Hopkins University Applied Physics Laboratory
Paul Dunn, Naval Undersea Warfare Center, Newport
Dave DeMartino, Naval Surface Warfare Center, Panama City
Barbara Fletcher, Space and Naval Warfare Systems Center, San Diego
Joe Hanlin, Fleet Support Activity Navy
Pat Madden, Johns Hopkins University Applied Physics Laboratory
Steve Mack, Facilitator – Navy Acquisition Center of Excellence (ACE)

Appendix D: Year 2004 UUV Master Plan Update Expert Panels

Core Study Team for year 2004 Navy UUV Master Plan Update:

The Core Team developing the update was a group of UUV experts from a range of Navy laboratories and academia. Team members included five of year 2000 team and were chosen for their extensive experience in UUV applications for mine countermeasures, anti-submarine warfare and training, search and salvage, tactical oceanography, surveillance, inspection, and undersea work.

Paul Dunn, Study Technical Director, Naval Undersea Warfare Center, Newport
Brad Burns, John Hopkins University Applied Physics Laboratory
Steve Castelin, Naval Surface Warfare Center, Panama City
Dave DeMartino, Naval Surface Warfare Center, Panama City
Steve Ebner, Naval Surface Warfare Center, Carderock
Barbara Fletcher, Space & Naval Warfare Systems Center, San Diego
Julia Gazagnaire, Naval Surface Warfare Center, Panama City
Ray Harnois, Naval Undersea Warfare Center, Newport
Sam Hester, Naval Undersea Warfare Center, Newport
Martha Head, Anteon, Inc. for Naval Meteorology and Oceanographic Command
George Kindel, Sonalysts, Inc.
John Lisiewicz, Naval Undersea Warfare Center, Newport
Pat Madden, Johns Hopkins University Applied Physics Laboratory
Steve Wells, Naval Surface Warfare Center, Carderock

Workshop 1:

LCDR Leif Bergey, Navy Warfare Development Command
Bob Brizzolara, Office of Naval Research 33X (Ship S&T Division)
James (Brad) Burns, John Hopkins University Applied Research Laboratory
CAPT (sel) Jerry Burroughs, PMS403
Paul Callahan, NAVSEA SEA 073
Steve Castelin, Naval Surface Warfare Center, Panama City
John Cooke, Naval Undersea Warfare Center Newport
Pierre Corriveau, Commander Submarine Force, U.S. Atlantic Fleet
Thomas Curtin, Office of Naval Research
Daniel Deitz, PMS403
Dave DeMartino, Naval Surface Warfare Center, Panama City
John Dudinski, Naval Surface Warfare Center, Panama City
Paul Dunn, Naval Undersea Warfare Center, Newport
Chris Egan, Naval Undersea Warfare Center, Newport
CAPT Dan Farson, Navy Warfare Development Command
Vic Fiebig, Defense Liaison Division - CNO
Barbara Fletcher, Space & Naval Warfare Systems Center, San Diego
Julia Gazagnaire, Naval Surface Warfare Center, Panama City
Al Goodman, Naval Undersea Warfare Center, Newport
Julio Gutierrez, Naval Undersea Warfare Center, Newport
LT Harper, Office of Naval Intelligence
Mike Harris, Naval Research Laboratory Code 7440
Martha Head, ANTEON Corp. (NAVOCEANO)

Sam Hester, Naval Undersea Warfare Center, Newport
Art Hommel, NAVSEA PEO (LMW) PMS403D
Charlene Bary Ingerson, Naval War College
Houston K. Jones, Space & Naval Warfare Systems Center, San Diego
CDR Paul Judice, Navy Warfare Development Command
ENS Robb S. Kellberg, Submarine Development Squadron FIVE Detachment UUV
George Kindel, Sonalysts Inc. (Naval Undersea Warfare Center, Newport)
Chief Brian Kulbeth, Submarine Development Squadron FIVE Detachment UUV
Tom Kyle, Commander Submarine Force, U.S. Pacific Fleet
Randy Large, Navy Special Warfare Group THREE
Bill Lonardo, Naval Undersea Warfare Center, Newport
CDR Thomas Lunney, Submarine Development Squadron FIVE
Pat Madden, John Hopkins University Applied Research Laboratory
LCDR Steve Martin, CNO N752K (Expeditionary Warfare Division)
David Medeiros, Naval Undersea Warfare Center, Newport
CAPT John C. Mickey, Naval Undersea Warfare Center, Newport
Joe Musich, Office of Naval Research/Naval Research Laboratory 107
Rick Nagle, EDO PSD (PMS_EOD)
CDR Richard Nicklas, OASN RDA (LMW)
LCDR Mike Nicklin, CNO-096/61 (Oceanographer of the Navy)
Jason Pawley, PMS420 (LCS Mission Modules)
Rich Peel, NUWC, Keyport, National UUV T&E Center (NUTEC)
CAPT Walter Pullar, NAVSEA PMS NSW
CAPT(sel) Randy Richards, CNO N778
CDR Anthony Rodgers, Naval Special Clearance Team ONE
Patricia Savage, AMS (PMS490)
Gary Smith, SPA
CDR Monty G. Spearman, NAVOCEANO
Lisa Tubridy, Naval Surface Warfare Center, Panama City
LCDR Vincent Vanoss, Office of Naval Intelligence, Deputy Director SWORD Division
Linda Wazlavek, OPNAV N763
Steve Wells, Naval Surface Warfare Center, Carderock
Cecil Whitfield, PEO LMW / PME 490CE

Workshop 2:
Dr. Brian S. Boureois, Naval Research Laboratory Code 7440.5
Bob Brizzolara, Office of Naval Research 33X (Ship S&T Division)
Todd Bruner, General Dynamics Advanced Information Systems
James (Brad) Burns, John Hopkins University Applied Research Laboratory
Steve Castelin, Naval Surface Warfare Center, Panama City
Pierre Corriveau, Commander, Submarine Force U.S. Atlantic Fleet
Jim Cranston, Electric Boat, General Dynamics
Jason Dalley, Office of Naval Intelligence
Nabil Daoud, The Boeing Company
LCDR Matt Dean, Submarine Development Squadron FIVE
Daniel Deitz, PMS403
Dave DeMartino, Naval Surface Warfare Center, Panama City

John Dudinski, Naval Surface Warfare Center, Panama City
Paul Dunn, Naval Undersea Warfare Center, Newport
Stephen Ebner, Naval Surface Warfare Center, Carderock
Vic Fiebig, Defense Liaison Division - CNO
CAPT Tracey A. Fischer, NAVSEA SEA 073
Barbara Fletcher, Space & Naval Warfare Systems Center, San Diego
Michael Fry, Northrop Grumman Newport News
Tim Gaffney, DASN Littoral & Mine Warfare
Dan Gallagher, Raytheon
LCDR Tim Gallaudet, Ph.D., COMNAVMETOCCOM
Julia Gazagnaire, Naval Surface Warfare Center, Panama City
William Girodet, Locheed Martin Maritime Sensors & Systems
Anthony Griffin, Office of Naval Intelligence
Julio Gutierrez, Naval Undersea Warfare Center, Newport
LT Rich Haas, Naval Special Clearance Team ONE
Martha Head, ANTEON Corp. (NAVOCEANO)
Sam Hester, Naval Undersea Warfare Center, Newport
Greg Hoffman, Naval War College
Art Hommel, NAVSEA PEO (LMW) PMS403D
Dr. John Huckabay, Applied Research Laboratory University of Texas
Stephen Hudson, Naval Surface Warfare Center, Panama City
CAPT Paul Ims, PEO LMW / PME 403
Charlene Bary Ingerson, Naval War College
Henry Jordan, BAE Systems (BIW)
LCDR Jeff Joseph, OPNAV N778C
ENS Robb S. Kellberg, Submarine Development Squadron FIVE Detachment UUV
LT Kennedy, NAVOCEANO Fleet Survey Team
Dan Kiely, Applied Research Laboratory, Pennsylvania State University
George Kindel, Sonalysts Inc. (Naval Undersea Warfare Center, Newport)
Steve Koepenick, Space & Naval Warfare Systems Center, San Diego
John Lademan, Northrop Grumman Oceanic Division
John Lathrop, Naval Surface Warfare Center, Panama City
John Lisiewicz, Naval Undersea Warfare Center, Newport
Charles Loeffler, Applied Research Laboratory, University of Texas
Pat Madden, John Hopkins University Applied Research Laboratory
Thomas Mallison, Applied Research Laboratory Pennsylvania State University
LCDR Steve Martin, CNO N752K (Expeditionary Warfare Division)
William Mathis, Raytheon Consultant
Ken McAdow, MITRE
Maria Medeiros, Naval Undersea Warfare Center, Newport
Mike Medeiros, Naval Undersea Warfare Center, Newport
Graham Mimpriss, NAVO Fleet Survey Team
William Moyer, Applied Research Laboratory Pennsylvania State University
Rob Murray, PMS-NSW
Dr. Dan Nagle, Naval Undersea Warfare Center, Newport
LCDR Mike Nicklin, CNO-096/61 (Oceanographer of the Navy)

Mack O'Brien, Draper Laboratory
Don Parker, Northrop Grumman Oceanic Division
Tom Pastore, SPAWARS San Diego
John Pavlos, Electric Boat, General Dynamics
Joel Peak, Naval Surface Warfare Center, Panama City
Tony Ruffa, Naval Undersea Warfare Center, Newport / Support PMS501
Guy Santora, Naval Surface Warfare Center, Panama City
Marian Savoie, Office of Naval Intelligence
Kenneth Sharp, Naval Oceanographic Office
Wade Sigstedt, Commander, Mine Warfare Command
Rob Simons, APM for EOD & Naval Special Clearance Team ONE UUV Programs
Gary Smith, SPA
CDR Monty G. Spearman, NAVOCEANO
Wayne Stamey, Office of Naval Intelligence
Thomas Swean, Office of Naval Research
Paul Temple, Naval Undersea Warfare Center, Newport
Lisa Tubridy, Naval Surface Warfare Center, Panama City
James Valentine, Naval Surface Warfare Center, Panama City
Christopher von Alt, Woods Hole Oceanographic Institute
Steve Wells, Naval Surface Warfare Center, Carderock
Cecil Whitfield, PEO LMW / PME 490CE
William F. Whitson, The Boeing Company
Scott Willcox, Bluefin Robotics Corp.
LT Jeff Yackeren, Submarine Development Squadron TWELVE

Workshop 3:
CAPT. Thomas Green, PMS-EOD
CAPT Paul Ims, PEO LMW / PME 403
Pat Madden, John Hopkins University Applied Physics Laboratory
CDR Monty G. Spearman, NAVOCEANO
John Benedict, John Hopkins University Applied Physics Laboratory
James (Brad) Burns, John Hopkins University Applied Physics Laboratory
Steve Castelin, Naval Surface Warfare Center, Panama City
Kevin Corcoran, Space & Naval Warfare Systems Center, San Diego
Dave DeMartino, Naval Surface Warfare Center, Panama City
Paul Dunn, Naval Undersea Warfare Center, Newport
Stephen Ebner, Naval Surface Warfare Center, Carderock
Chris Egan, Naval Undersea Warfare Center, Newport
Vic Fiebig, Defense Liaison Division - CNO
Barbara Fletcher, Space & Naval Warfare Systems Center, San Diego
LCDR Tim Gallaudet, Ph.D., COMNAVMETOCCOM
Julia Gazagnaire, Naval Surface Warfare Center, Panama City
Ray M. Harnois, Naval Undersea Warfare Center, Newport
Martha Head, ANTEON Corp. (NAVOCEANO)
Dr. Beth S. Hester, NAVOCEANO
Sam Hester, Naval Undersea Warfare Center, Newport

Harry Hogenkamp, The MITRE Corp.
Art Hommel, NAVSEA PEO (LMW) PMS403D
George Kindel, Sonalysts Inc. (Naval Undersea Warfare Center, Newport)
Don Kluberdanz, Naval Undersea Warfare Center, Newport
John Lisiewicz, Naval Undersea Warfare Center Newport
LCDR Steve Martin, CNO N752K (Expeditionary Warfare Division)
Dennis McLaughlin, Naval Undersea Warfare Center, Newport
Paul Milcetic, PMS-EOD
RADM J. Brad Mooney, USN (Ret.),
Rob Murray, PMS-NSW
LCDR Mike Nicklin, CNO-096/61 (Oceanographer of the Navy)
Jim Oblinger, Naval Undersea Warfare Center NPT
Andy Pedersen, Naval EOD Technology Division
Rich Peel, NUWC Keyport, National UUV T&E Center (NUTEC)
Bill Schoenster, PEO (Ships) PMS501M
Dr. John Short, Naval Undersea Warfare Center, Newport
Bryan Tollefson, Space & Naval Warfare Systems Center, San Diego
Steve Wells, Naval Surface Warfare Center, Carderock

Appendix E: Year 2004 UUV Master Plan Update Workshops

A series of three workshops was held to gather inputs from Navy users, stakeholders, Navy laboratories, academia, and industry. Decision support (GroupSystems) software was used to gather and prioritize workshop attendee input.

Picture E-1 shows the process flow, including how the workshops were used in the update process, and the following sections provide additional detail on each workshop.

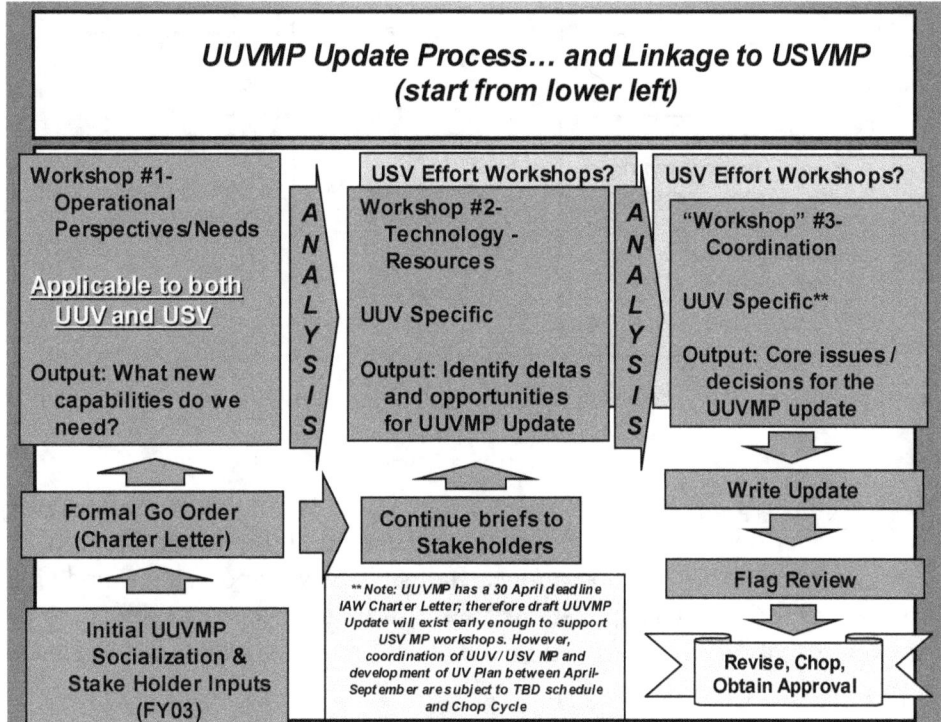

Picture E-1. UUVMP Update Workshop Process Flow

Workshop 1

The purpose of Workshop 1 was to review the current UUV Master Plan and high-level Navy guidance, receive briefs on current and future threats, and then capture participant inputs on potential UUV missions. Picture E-1 summarizes the agenda and process used. Following the briefings, the workshop participants grouped and prioritized the selected missions.

Following the mission prioritization, the UUV missions were sorted into the subsets of Sea Power 21 pillars. These UUV missions came to be known as "Sub-Pillars" for the remainder of the project, as shown in Picture E-2.

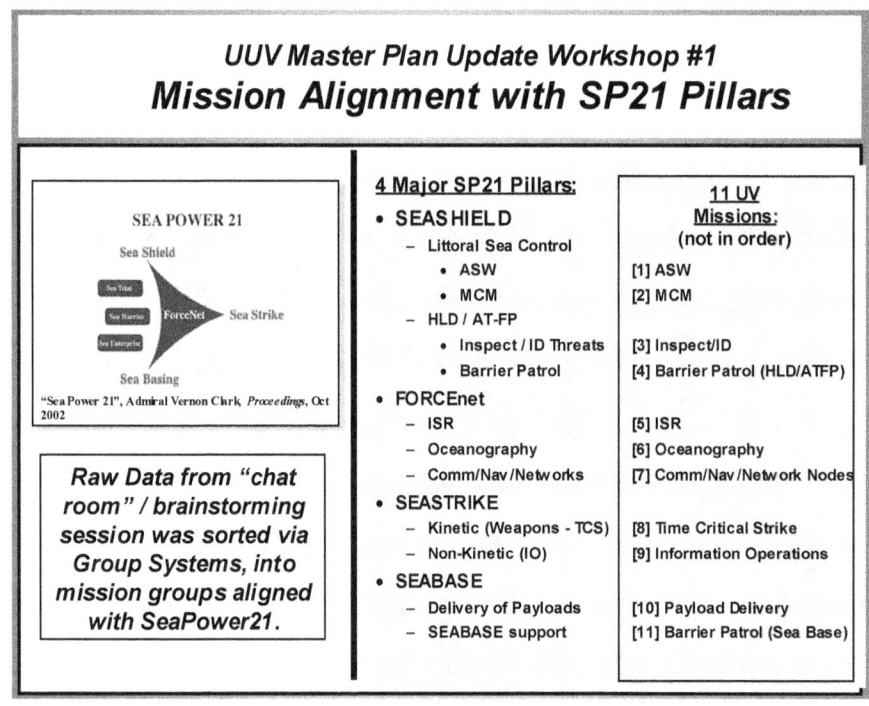

Picture E-2. UUV Mission Alignment

Workshop 2

The purpose of Workshop 2 was to review current UUV technologies and identify gaps and opportunities for further development. Briefs were received on threats and lessons learned from actual UUV peacetime and wartime operations. Industry, Navy laboratories, and ONR also gave a series of technology briefs. GroupSystems voting was again used to prioritize the identified UUV missions and capability gaps with this new set of attendees. Picture E-3 summarizes the Workshop 2 process.

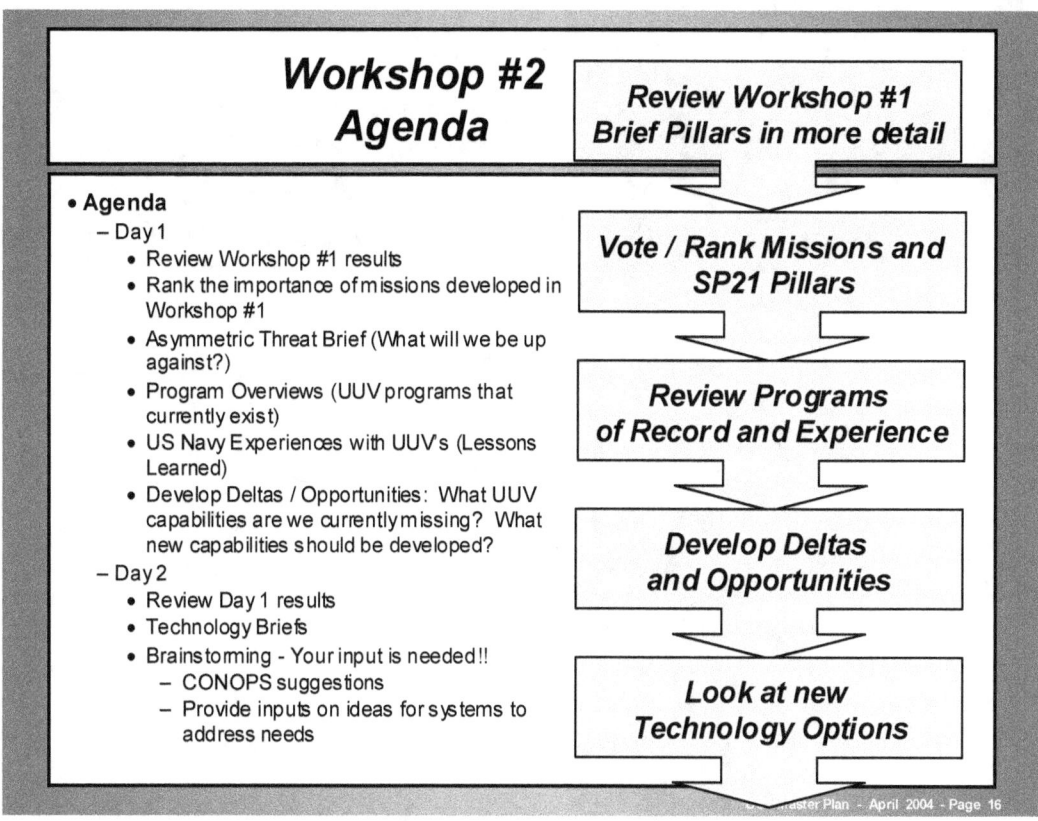

Picture E-3. UUVMP Update Workshop 2 Agenda

Workshop 3

The purpose of Workshop 3 was to review the results of the two previous workshops, identify core issues and make key decisions for executing the UUV Master Plan Update. Presentations were given on FORCEnet, Undersea FORCEnet, UUV Standards, platform interfaces, platform mission modules, USVs, and UUV related Analysis of Alternatives (AoA) studies. GroupSystems discussions were used to help determine which missions are best performed by UUVs and which could be better performed by other manned or unmanned platforms. Following Workshop 3, the Study Team began developing a roadmap for Navy UUV systems.

Process Summary

As delineated above, the UUV Master Plan Study Team conducted a thorough review of high-level Navy guidance, existing UUV programs, technology availability and Fleet need. The Team developed a set of eleven major UUV missions based on articulated Fleet needs, and then categorized these missions as "Sub-Pillars" of Sea Power 21 Pillars. Additional analyses, both in a GroupSystems setting with invited guest experts and by the Study Team, resulted in filtering of the missions for technical feasibility, evaluation of appropriateness for UUVs, and establishment of priorities.   Two missions, Barrier Patrol for Homeland Defense / Anti-Terrorism Force Protection and for Sea Base Support, were removed from first-tier consideration. All missions are discussed in Chapter 2 Section 2.3, and the nine prioritized missions are discussed in more detail in Chapter 3.